WHEN JESUS CONFRONTS
THE WORLD

WHEN JESUS CONFRONTS THE WORLD

An Exposition of Matthew 8 – 10

D.A. Carson

Authentic

British Library Cataloguing-in-Publication Data

A catalogue record for this book is available from the
British Library

ISBN 978-1-85078-890-4

Cover design by Philip Miles
Printed and bound in Great Britain by
CPI Cox & Wyman, Reading, RG1 8EX

Contents

Preface

My parents were both born in the United Kingdom: my mother was born a Cockney, my father entered this world just outside Belfast. In the providence of God, I spent several years in doctoral research in England, and at the end of that time, I married an Englishwoman. Owing to the generous sabbatical and study leave system at Trinity Evangelical Divinity School, I have kept returning to Cambridge every so often, drawn not least by the excellent facilities of Tyndale House and the University Library.

One of the strongest attractions to Cambridge for our family, however, is the tie with Eden Baptist Church. In some ways that is our church home. Our family owes our brothers and sisters in that church a debt of gratitude that extends back over a decade and a half. So when we knew we were returning to Cambridge for the 1986–87 academic year, and the invitation came to use the first six weeks of my sabbatical filling the Eden pulpit while its pastor, Dr Roy Clements, was finishing up his own sabbatical, I was in no position to decline, and was delighted to fill in.

In any case, I was a pastor long before I started pursuing more academic forms of service; and I am deeply persuaded that those of us whose privilege and responsibility it is to study the Scriptures owe the church whatever help we can give at the popular level, quite apart from the responsibility of producing work that attempts to influence teachers and scholars. If the purpose of my sabbatical was to complete a syntactical concordance to the Greek New Testament, there needed to be space as well for something that served the church more immediately.

I first expounded the New Testament chapters treated in this little book, Matthew 8 – 10, fifteen years ago in the course of pastoral ministry on the west coast of Canada. In the intervening years I have written a full-length commentary on Matthew (in *The Expositor's Bible Commentary*, vol. 8); I hope my grasp of the text is a little firmer now than when I first preached on these chapters. Because I have discussed critical and interpretative questions at some length in that commentary, I have avoided raising such issues here, and for the same reason have not included bibliography and notes. The sermon is not the place for unloading that sort of information in any case. But by comparing the commentary with this exposition, seminary students may obtain some impression of how at least one person tries to move from detailed exegesis to the exposition of the Word of God.

The six chapters in this book, then, are sermons that have been reworked for the printed page. Not all traces of the sermon have been removed. In particular, the application of Scripture that characterizes all useful preaching has been retained; but a number of forms suitable to the pulpit have undergone a metamorphosis to become suitable to the written essay. Occasionally I have added a trifle more explanation or other detail than the constraints of the sermons allowed.

I would like to thank Baker Book House for adding this book to the series of expositions they have already published. Not every publisher is willing to print sermons, reworked or otherwise. That they have done so testifies to their awareness of one of the great needs of the church: the need to read the Bible in a way that simultaneously understands what the text is actually saying, and applies it fairly and closely to our own lives and to the world around us. If we lose the first of these two poles, we never hear the Word of God; if we lose the second, the Word never sings or stings.

If this little book contributes in a small way to meeting this need, I shall be grateful to God.

Soli Deo gloria.

D.A. Carson
Trinity Evangelical Divinity School

1 (Matthew 8:1–17)

The Authority of Jesus

When he came down from the mountainside, large crowds followed him. A man with leprosy came and knelt before him and said, 'Lord, if you are willing, you can make me clean.'

Jesus reached out his hand and touched the man. 'I am willing,' he said. 'Be clean!' Immediately he was cured of his leprosy. Then Jesus said to him, 'See that you don't tell anyone. But go, show yourself to the priest and offer the gift Moses commanded, as a testimony to them.'

When Jesus had entered Capernaum, a centurion came to him, asking for help. 'Lord,' he said, 'my servant lies at home paralyzed and in terrible suffering.'

Jesus said to him, 'I will go and heal him.'

The centurion replied, 'Lord, I do not deserve to have you come under my roof. But just say the word, and my servant will be healed. For I myself am a man under authority, with soldiers under me. I tell this one, "Go," and he goes; and that one, "Come," and he comes. I say to my servant, "Do this," and he does it.'

When Jesus heard this, he was astonished and said to those following him, 'I tell you the truth, I have not found anyone in Israel with such great faith. I say to you that many will come from the east and the west, and will take their places at the feast with Abraham, Isaac and Jacob in the kingdom of heaven. But the subjects of the kingdom will be thrown outside, into the darkness, where there will be weeping and gnashing of teeth.'

Then Jesus said to the centurion, 'Go! It will be done just as you believed it would.' And his servant was healed at that very hour.

When Jesus came into Peter's house, he saw Peter's mother-in-law lying in bed with a fever. He touched her hand and the fever left her, and she got up and began to wait on him.

When evening came, many who were demon-possessed were brought to him, and he drove out the spirits with a word and healed all the sick. This was to fulfil what was spoken through the prophet Isaiah:

'He took up our infirmities
and carried our diseases.'

Introduction

I

Certain confrontations inevitably arouse the expectation that there will be an explosion. The media know this best, of course; and that is why whenever they interview a representative of some position or other, they almost invariably try to find a foil, a representative of another position, one that is diametrically opposed to the first. Their aim, of course, is to bring the two positions into confrontation, knowing that the resulting explosion makes good press.

The principle can be grasped intuitively. Take a deeply committed Marxist and an avowed capitalist and ask each to explain to an audience the reasons for the high levels of British unemployment – and what is the result? It is not simply that one side will blame the history of social welfarism and the lack of incentive while the other will point to the economic and social stratification of British society, but that the exchange may generate emotional and colourful charges and countercharges. Maroon a militant atheist and a zealous fundamentalist on a desert island for a few weeks, or put a television camera before an ardent feminist and a reactionary male chauvinist, and you achieve the same result. The confrontation arouses expectations of an explosion, or at least of an extremely revealing encounter.

Something similar can be expected when Jesus confronts the world. I use the word world in its larger, theological sense – the created, moral order in rebellion against God its Maker. In the Bible, this sense of 'world' is much favoured by John. For instance, he warns us, 'Do not love the world or anything in the world. If anyone loves the world, the love of the Father is not in him. For everything in the world – the cravings of sinful man, the lust of his eyes and the boasting of what he has and does – comes not from the Father but from the world. The world and its desires pass away, but the man who does the will of God lives forever' (1 John 2:15–17). When Jesus confronts the world in this sense of 'world,' some kind of explosion can be expected; for Jesus and the world are very different, frankly opposite in their purpose, character, values, and aims. The world is essentially self-centered; Jesus did not come to be served, but to serve, and to give his life a ransom for many (Matt. 20:28). The world is in active rebellion against God; Jesus always pleases his Father (John 8:29). The world (as we have just seen in the quotation from John) is time-bound and temporary; not so Jesus or his kingdom or the

person who does his will. The world needs saving, and
Jesus comes to save his people from their sins (Matt.
1:21); the world needs judging, and Jesus is the Son of
man who comes when least expected and passes the
entire world under review (Matt. 24:36 – 25:46). Jesus
and the world are bound to clash with each other.

That is one reason why even those closest to Jesus in
the days of his flesh took a long time to understand him:
they were much more in league with the world than
they understood, so much participants in the world that
they did not grasp the nature of the confrontation taking
place. Thus when Peter in Matthew 16 confesses Jesus to
be the Messiah, he does so only because the Father has
revealed the point to him: the implication seems to be
that apart from such revelation Peter would have been
unable to come to this conclusion. And immediately
after his great confession, Peter, confusing Jesus' explanation of this fact with a compliment, thinks he is in a
position to correct Jesus as to the nature of his mission,
and earns the rebuke, 'Get behind me, Satan! You are a
stumbling block to me; you do not have in mind the
things of God, but the things of men' (Matt. 16:23). Peter
was far more attached to the world than he knew.

In the same way, men and women today do not
always recognize the nature of the confrontation
between Jesus and the world, precisely because they are
more deeply bound up in allegiance to the world than
they think. Many people, of course, openly admit they
have nothing to do with Jesus; but others believe they
deserve a very high place in the moral scheme of things
and that they are therefore principally in league with
Jesus, 'Christians,' even if they are not, say, church-
goers. These people have not begun to comprehend the
gulf that separates them from Jesus; when the claims
and demands of the biblical Jesus are pressed on them,

they take offence and go away in a huff. Still others are active followers of Jesus, as was Peter, but their allegiance is still warped by exaggerated estimates of their own spiritual insight and wisdom. They are more deeply impregnated by the wisdom of the world than they think. When they find out more about the real Jesus, painful confrontation is part of the price as they examine the foundations once more.

In the three chapters before us, Matthew 8 – 10, we are presented with a number of things that transpire when Jesus confronts the world. Some of these are quite wonderful: the healings and exorcisms (8:16–17; 9:32–33), and the assurance that Jesus has come to call sinners (9:13). Others are frankly frightening: Jesus' teaching that some who expect to inherit the kingdom are 'thrown outside, into the darkness, where there will be weeping and gnashing of teeth' (8:12); his insistence that his mission entails the active disruption of family units as people are forced to choose between family and him (10:34–36). Still others are simply startling: Jesus' rather shocking response to the disciple who wants to suspend following Jesus until he has buried his father ('Follow me, and let the dead bury their own dead' [8:22]). And some are alarming to sincere followers of Jesus, especially the assurance of opposition and persecution (10:16,22,37–39). But always there is confrontation, explicit or implict.

Yet if we think our way carefully through these chapters, they will serve to focus a number of characteristics of Jesus, the way a lens gathers light and focuses it into a beam. The confrontation between Jesus and the world helps to clarify the nature of both Jesus and the world. As a result, we gain understanding of who Jesus is and who we are; we are forced to choose, forced to assess whether our allegiance is to Jesus or to the world, and driven to understand the nature of the confrontation between Jesus and the world two thousand years ago. And in that understanding we find the structures that enable us to comprehend the nature of the confrontation between Jesus and the world today.

II

I have grouped some of the things we learn about Jesus from his confrontation with the world into themes that will be treated chapter by chapter in this book. The first of these concerns the authority of Jesus.

What comes to mind when we use the word *authority*? The answer depends entirely on the context. Consider these six statements:

1.*Professor Smith is the world's leading* authority *on the duck-billed platypus.* This does not necessarily mean that Professor Smith is a good man, or that everything he says about the duck-billed platypus is true, or that there is no one who knows more about certain restricted aspects of the platypus than Professor Smith. Rather, it means that no one knows more about the duck-billed platypus than does Professor Smith. Perhaps he has written the major textbook on the subject; all other learning on the topic will be measured by his.

2. *The president of the United States has the* authority *to dismiss the secretary of state.* This means that the president, by virtue of the office he holds, can take a certain action (firing the secretary of state). No one can prevent the president from taking this action if he is determined upon it. This authority cannot be contested. Unlike the use of 'authority' in the first sentence, this use does not depend on superior knowledge but on rank, a particular office.

3. The prime minister has delegated to her press secretary the authority *to speak to the media on her behalf.* Here authority is delegated (unlike the first two uses). The person to whom this authority is delegated must use that authority responsibly, or face disciplinary action.

4. All of us love to tweak the nose of the authorities. Here the word authority has as its referent not a concept but people – people who exercise certain authority. In this context we conjure up officials who are not as grand or as important as they think they are, and whose pretensions are amusingly burst by some mild fun.

5. His problem is that he likes to stand on his authority. This use is much like the previous one, except that the humor has evaporated to leave the smell of pompous hypocrisy. Here the bureaucrat is confusing personal importance with the rights of office. Such authority depends not on knowledge (use 1) but on an abuse of raw power. It cannot be delegated: indeed, a person who loves to stand on his own authority would not want to delegate it.

6. In the midst of Watergate, President Nixon lost much of his authority. Of course in one sense as long as Nixon remained president he did not lose any of this authority: he enjoyed the full panoply of presidential powers. But in fact he lost a certain moral authority. Congress fought him on everything; every statement he made was viewed with grave suspicion and quoted as evidence of his moral delinquency. The kind of authority he lost was not bound up with his office but with his person, with the public perception of his integrity and credibility. A person may enjoy such authority without holding any office; and the authority of office cannot ever replace or be confused with this moral authority.

The reason this discussion is important to the passage before us is that Matthew 8 – 10 are linked with the Sermon on the Mount (Matt. 5 – 7) through the crucial verses at the end of chapter 7: 'When Jesus had finished saying these things [i.e., the utterances of chaps. 5 – 7], the crowds were amazed at his teaching, because he taught as one who had *authority*, and not as their teachers of the law' (7:28–29; emphasis added). We must ask what kind of authority Jesus was exercising. The crowds were amazed in part at the *center* of his authority. Many of the teachers of the law proceeded by citing other authorities (not unlike the modern thesis that is no more than a learned recitation of current opinion, complete with endless footnotes); but Jesus said again and again, 'You have heard that it was said . . . but *I* tell you . . .' (5:21ff.; emphasis added). In this regard he is not even like an Old Testament prophet who cries, 'Thus says the Lord!' He dares to speak with an authoritative 'I.'

But there is more to Jesus' authority in the Sermon on the Mount than the forms of his speech. He claims to determine who does and who does not enter the kingdom: 'Not everyone who says *to me*, "Lord, Lord," will enter the kingdom of heaven, but only he who does the will of my Father who is in heaven. Many will say to me on that day, "Lord, Lord, did we not prophesy *in your name*, and *in your name* drive out demons and perform many miracles?" Then *I* will tell them plainly, "*I* never knew you. Away from *me*, you evildoers!"' (7:21–23; emphases added). The true heirs of the kingdom, he insisted, would be persecuted because of their allegiance to him (5:11); and indeed he himself has come to fulfil the Old Testament law and prophets (5:17–20). They point to *him*, they anticipate *him*; but that means *he* is *in his own perception* greater in significance than they are.

Small wonder that the crowds are impressed with Jesus' self-conscious authority, even if they do not rightly assess it or understand it. But then Matthew, having drawn our attention to Jesus' authority in his teaching ministry, goes on in chapters 8 – 10 to display Jesus' authority as it is demonstrated in powerful deeds as well as in powerful words. Matthew groups together a series of healings, miracles of nature, the driving out of unclean spirits, and finally even the delegation of some of this authority to his disciples (chap. 10). In this light, then, these three chapters are suffused with Jesus' authority.

And what is the nature of this authority? Here is authority that has a moral center and is always effective. Power is bound up with this authority: there is no mere semblance of vigor, but such awesome capability that even Jesus' words are effective. Like the Sermon on the Mount, those parts of these chapters reflecting Jesus' teaching display the authority of the expert – but unlike Professor Smith of duck-billed platypus fame, Jesus' expertise in the matters he discusses cannot be gainsaid or set aside, for among mortals there is no one qualified to challenge his teaching. At least some of his authority can be delegated to his disciples (10:1); yet he remains qualitatively above them, in his integrity unimpeachable, in his authority peerless. Never is this authority stuffy or arrogant, for its locus is a Savior whose mission is to serve, to die, to help, to heal, to transform. If (ghastly thought) someone should for a dark moment entertain the desire to tweak the nose of this authority, the temptation would quickly be displaced by shame.

The Authority of Jesus

From the first seventeen verses of Matthew 8, we learn five things about the authority of Jesus.

1. The authority of Jesus to heal and transform is implicit in his person and mission (8:1–3). In a general way, this point is best drawn from the array of Jesus' miracles scattered throughout the Gospels. The prophet Isaiah had foreseen a time when the wolf would live with the lamb, when the leopard would lie down with the goat, when the calf and the lion and the yearling would live happily together, and a little child would lead them; when an infant could play safely near a cobra's hole or put his hand into a viper's nest; when no one would harm or destroy others, and when the earth, would be full of the knowledge of the Lord as the waters cover the sea (Isa. 11). The Messiah would be sent to preach good news to the poor, to bind up the brokenhearted, to proclaim freedom for the captives and release for the prisoners, to proclaim the year of the Lord's favour, to comfort those who mourn, to bestow on those who grieve a crown of beauty instead of ashes, the oil of gladness instead of mourning, and a garment of praise instead of a spirit of despair – as well as to declare the day of vengeance of our God (Isa. 61). The Old Testament Scriptures preserve many such prophecies, and the miracles of Jesus bring at least some of these prophecies to fulfilment.

When John the Baptist entertains doubts about who Jesus is, Jesus himself replies in words deeply reminiscent of Isaiah 61: 'Go back and report to John what you hear and see: The blind receive sight, the lame walk, those who have leprosy are cured, the deaf hear, the dead are raised, and the good news is preached to the poor. Blessed is the man who does not fall away on account of me' (Matt. 11:4–6). In other words, Jesus' ministry of power, displayed in his miracles, constituted evidence of his ident-ity as the promised Messiah. Perhaps the Baptist entertained doubts because while he lay languishing in prison he longed to see a little more of 'the day of vengeance of our God'; but whether or not that was the factor that drove him to doubt, the focus of Jesus' response to him is plain enough: the miracles that Jesus performs attest who he is and the mission he was sent to accomplish.

But this general point, which can be deduced from the record of Jesus' miracles as a whole, is greatly stressed in the miracle of healing the leper (8:1–3). The point is made three ways.

First, the disease itself (whether it was what modern medicine calls leprosy [Hansen's disease] or some other skin ailment) was greatly abhorred and feared by the Jews; and its cure was considered a singular mark of God's intervention. Those who contracted the disease were forced to live apart, isolated from human touch and the joys of intimate human contact. To be a leper often meant you were under God's curse (see Num. 12:10,12; Job 18:13). Healings were rare (see Num. 12:10–15; 2 Kgs. 5:9–14) and were sometimes thought to be as difficult as raising the dead (2 Kgs. 5:7,14). Jesus himself understood the healing of leprosy to be a mark of the dawning of the messianic age (Matt. 11:5). Probably that is why Matthew places this account at the head of his list of healings: it provides a startlingly powerful instance of Jesus' authority at work.

Second, Jesus' act of touching the leper (8:3) is more than a raw historical reminiscence. A leper would not have dared to touch someone who was not a leper; the person who touched a leper was judged ceremonially unclean, quite apart from the danger of contracting the disease. How this leper worked his way through the 'large crowds' (8:1), which at this stage dogged every step of Jesus' ministry, is not clear: perhaps he gave warning cries or rang a bell, and the crowd split around him until he could kneel before Jesus. But Jesus 'reached out his hand and touched the man.' It may have been the first human touch the leper had known for a long time.

Mark explains that Jesus was moved by compassion. He could have healed with a word, avoiding touch; but Jesus touched what others would have found repulsive. Yet the important thing to note is that Jesus does not thereby become unclean, but the leper becomes clean! When Jesus comes in contact with defilement, he is never defiled. Far from it: his touch has the power to cleanse defilement.

Third, the words by which the leper addresses Jesus are immensely significant: 'Lord, if you are willing, you can make me clean' (v. 2). Jesus replies, 'I am willing . . . Be clean!' (v. 3).This exchange does not call in question Jesus' general willingness to do good, as if he has to be coerced into kindness. Rather, both the leper's statement and Jesus' response to it frankly recognize that Jesus already has the authority and the power to perform the healing; all that is needed is his decision to act, and the healing takes place. Jesus' authority is here stressed by presupposing it.

This is one of the ways in which Jesus' healing ministry is rather different from that of the Old Testament prophets Elijah and Elisha. They too act and speak with authority; but the total impression deflects attention away from themselves and toward God. Although Jesus is concerned to glorify the Father, nevertheless there is a self-conscious awareness of the center of authority in his own teaching and healings absent from any other person in Scripture. In this passage, the healing of the leper turns on Jesus' will, nothing else: 'I am willing' – and the matter is settled. 'Go!' he says to the demons (8:32), and they are thereby released to invade the swine. 'Your sins are forgiven' (9:2) – and they are remembered no more.

'Get up, take your mat and go home' (9:6) – and the paralytic walks.

The authority of Jesus to heal and transform is implicit in his person and mission. The authority is *already* his. He needs only to will the deed, and it is done. Few lessons are more urgently needed in the modern church. Hope for reformation and revival lies not in campaigns and strategy (as important as such things may be), but in the authority of Jesus. His followers must come to him with the attitude of the leper in this account: they must recognize the sweep of his authority and petition him for grace, for a decision to display his authority in their favour.

We can best understand what this involves when we contrast the leper's request for a miracle with requests that Jesus spurns. In Matthew 12:38 and 16:1 certain religious leaders approach Jesus and ask him to perform a miraculous sign; but they earn only rebuke from the Master. They had not asked from the perspective of personal need, nor even from the vantage point of the supplicant. Rather, they ask Jesus for a sign in order that they might come to believe him. They thus set themselves up as judges, not needy folk hungry for grace. There was ample opportunity to witness Jesus' miracles; but they wanted a miracle on demand. If Jesus had complied, he would have been compromised, a trained stuntman programmed to perform tricks on command. The religious leaders would have domesticated him. That is why he rejects their challenge so decisively. The invading power of the kingdom is at Jesus' disposal, not theirs. It is *his* will that is decisive, not theirs. To avail oneself of Jesus' transforming power, one must come as a humble petitioner in need – or not at all.

Our generation is in danger of forgetting this. Even with regard to healing, opinion is polarized. One faction is persuaded there can be no miraculous healings today, as if the dawning of the kingdom ceased when Jesus returned to glory, not to be manifest again until he returns. Another faction treats healing as a sovereign right, to be gained by the appropriate manipulation of formulae. Both sides are in danger of trying to domesticate Jesus. I shall return to this subject in the last point of this chapter.

More broadly, the church is closest to heaven-sent revival when it comes to an end of its gimmicks, and petitions the great Lord of the church, who alone has the authority to pour out blessing beyond what can be imagined, who alone opens doors such that none can shut them and shuts them so that none can open them, to use the full authority that is his (Matt. 28:18) to bless his people with repentance and vitality and thereby bring glory to himself. Only his authority will suffice.

2. *The authority of Jesus, formally submissive to the law of Moses, in fact transcends it and fulfills it (8:4).* Why Jesus forbids the healed leper from telling anyone, Matthew does not make immediately clear. But if we may judge from parallel situations, one of the prime purposes Jesus has in this and similar prohibitions is to discourage the notion that he is primarily a wonderworker who can be pressed into messiahship by enthusiastic crowds more interested in healings, bread, and trouncing the Romans than in righteousness, repentance, and revelation from the Father. Jesus' authority derives from God alone; it is not dependent on the will of the people. Jesus can never be a democratically elected Messiah. The will of the people is often fickle; and in any case it is usually controlled by what the people think they can get, not by how eagerly they will submit. The parallels (Mark 1:45; Luke 5:15) tell us that the healed leper disobeyed Jesus, and spread the

news of his cure far and wide, ultimately hampering Jesus' ministry and forcing him to retire to wilderness areas away from the major centres of population. Those details are not related by Matthew; but he records enough of Jesus' injunctions to be silent that we may be sure he is not unaware of the danger.

But if Jesus will not be submissive to the will of the crowds, it appears at first glance that he is submissive to the Scripture, and to the law of Moses in particular. Leviticus 14 provides detailed information on what the person is to do who believes himself healed of leprosy. The final decision as to whether or not healing has taken place is in the hand of the priest; a lengthy ritual is prescribed involving delay, careful inspection, and finally a sin offering to 'make atonement for the one to be cleansed from his uncleanness' (Lev. 14:19). That is the passage Jesus is thinking of when he tells the leper, now cured, 'But go, show yourself to the priest and offer the gift Moses commanded' (Matt. 8:4). Indeed, in every particular Jesus was quick to show himself submissive to the written law of God. To use Paul's words, he was 'born under law'; and throughout his earthly pilgrimage he remained faithful to that calling.

Nevertheless, the closing words of the verse show there is more to this prescription from the law of Moses than first meets the eye. 'But go,' Jesus tells the cured leper, 'show yourself to the priest and offer the gift Moses commanded, *as a testimony to them.*' The expression used in the original could be taken to mean 'as a testimony *for* them,' that is, to help them to come to faith; or 'as a testimony *against* them,' that is, as a kind of denunciation of their unbelief. Of the places where the expression is used in the synoptic Gospels, however, in only two instances is it clearly negative; usually it is neutral.[1] In other words, Jesus wants the cured leper's obedience to the law to serve as a witness; whether it will prove a positive witness and an incentive to faith, or a negative witness that exposes the depth of unbelief, is not specified in the expression and will be revealed only in the response to the witness.

In fact, debate over whether this witness is meant to be positive or negative has sometimes distracted us from its truly startling feature. *Of what* would this 'gift,' this sacrifice that the cured leper would offer, serve as a witness? In the context, clearly it would serve as a witness to the fact that the man was healed – and healed by the transforming power of Jesus, who is relating his power to his messianic calling and mission. Thus the law of Moses itself is being used to testify to who Jesus is. In other words, in this context the supreme function of the gift Moses commanded (Lev. 14:10–18) is not as a guilt offering but as a witness to Jesus. In his very act of submission to the law, Jesus makes the law point to himself. If the cured leper pursues the various steps laid out by Moses to attest his purification, then the priest must pronounce him clean; and the pronouncement attests that Jesus performed the miracle that brought about the cleanness. And whereas that does not *prove* Jesus is the Messiah, it does provide attestation that must be taken seriously.

This is a minor but still important example of the way the New Testament writers rather consistently spell out the relationship between Jesus and the old covenant. Already in the Sermon on the Mount Jesus has insisted that he did not come to abolish the law *but to fulfill it* – which does not mean to intensify it, or to show its deeper legal and moral significance, or the like, but quite literally to fulfil it. The presupposition is that the law can be viewed as prophetic; and that to which it points is Jesus and his gospel. The law points to Jesus, prepares the way for him, provides models of sacrifice that find their antitype in him, prescribes morality that finds its apex and best exemplar in him, demands holiness that only he can provide, and generally anticipates him. As Jesus later insists, both the law and the prophets prophesied (Matt. 11:13) – sometimes in prepositional forms, sometimes in types, sometimes as part of a matrix that pointed ahead (as Paul in Gal. 3, and the writer to the Hebrews throughout his book, insist).

This theme is so pervasive in the New Testament that it would take a very large book even to begin to expound it adequately. But the crucial conclusion from our point of view is that Jesus is presented in the Bible not as an auxiliary figure who complements other notables such as Moses and David and Jeremiah, but as the focal point of God's revelation. As the Epistle to the Hebrews puts it, God had spoken to the fathers by the prophets; but in these last days he has spoken to us in his Son (Heb. 1:1–3). The 'word of God' did indeed come to the prophets; but at a deeper level the Son himself is the Word par excellence, God's Self-Expression. To use the language of the apostle John, this Word, this Self-Expression of God, has always been with God and is in fact God (John 1:1); but this Self-Expression of God became flesh (John 1:14), enabling us to see his glory. The apex of God's gracious self-disclosure is in Jesus.

As much as it is true that Jesus obeyed the law of Moses, his claims insisted that he stood over it – as its fulfilment (Matt. 5:17), as the Lord of the Sabbath (12:8), as the one to whom the law witnesses (8:4). His authority is astounding, and calls from his followers the reverence of worship and obedience.

3. *The authority of Jesus is so sweeping that when Jesus speaks, God speaks (8:5–9).* Centurions constituted the

military backbone of the Roman Empire. Unlike the senior officers, they went over the wall with their troops. They exercised discipline, trained the recruits, carried out orders from higher up. At this point there were probably no Roman centurions in Palestine. Most likely this one was recruited from a neighbouring territory such as Lebanon or Syria. Elsewhere we learn of his Jewish sympathies and friends; in Matthew's brief account, the emphasis is on his race and his faith (8:10–11).

This centurion's approach to Jesus is astonishing in its humility and its display of faith. At the risk of casting slurs, one must admit that centurions do not normally treat representatives of conquered peoples with utmost respect. Yet here is a Roman centurion treating Jesus, one of the conquered Jews, as if he were of a rank so exalted that the humble home of the soldier was not suitable for him. There is no suggestion in the text that the centurion was simply providing a way for Jesus to escape ceremonial defilement. Rather, he felt his unworthiness before Jesus and with becoming humility approached the Master on behalf of his suffering servant. In this attitude he joins with the leper in a stance described by the first beatitude: 'Blessed are the poor in spirit, for theirs is the kingdom of heaven' (5:3). Grace answers to unpretentious need, but to neither smug self-confidence nor pretentious and bombastic breast-beating.

But more surprising is the telling power of the illustration the centurion uses when he asks Jesus simply to perform the healing miracle with a word, instead of coming to pray over the servant and perhaps lay hands on him. Just 'say the word, and my servant will be healed,' the centurion petitions. 'For I myself am a man under authority, with soldiers under me. I tell this one, "Go," and he goes; and that one, "Come,"and he comes. I say to my servant, "Do this," and he does it' (8:8–11).

The centurion sees himself as simultaneously *under* authority and as one *exercising* authority: 'I myself,' he says, 'am a man under authority, with soldiers under me.' In the Roman military system, all ultimate authority was vested in the emperor and was delegated down the military hierarchy. Therefore, because he was a part of this structure, when the centurion commanded a foot soldier to come or go or do something, he was not speaking as one man to another but as a representative of Rome. The centurion was under the authority of his commanding tribune, and so on all the way back to the emperor; but the foot soldier was under him. Therefore when the centurion spoke, so far as those under him were concerned it was Rome that was speaking. Disobedience to the centurion was not mere defiance of a fellow human being, but rebellion against Rome, treason before the emperor, an insult to the empire.

The centurion applies to Jesus this grasp of his own position and authority. Because Jesus is under God's authority, always perfectly conforming to the authority that is exercised over him, the centurion is certain that when Jesus exercises authority it is none less than God's authority. When the centurion speaks, Rome speaks; when Jesus speaks, God speaks. To defy Jesus is to defy God. Jesus' word is invested with God's authority; so   he is well able to heal sickness with a word. When the centurion gives commands to those under him, things happen: he does not have to be there to oversee every step of the operation, because he is conscious of the authority vested in him, and his word is sufficient to guarantee that the operation is carried out. He expects no less from Jesus: if when Jesus speaks he exercises the authority of God himself, there is no real need for Jesus to be present or to check up on the result. The word itself is authoritative and cannot be ineffective. If Jesus but commands the sickness to cease, it will cease.

Like all analogies, this one is not perfect; nonetheless, the centurion's argument reveals an astonishing level of faith that recognizes that the powerful deeds Jesus was performing did not turn on magic, ritual, or subterfuge, but on his *authority*, which was nothing other than the authority of God himself. His word would be effective because it was God's word.

4. *The authority of Jesus is a great comfort to the eyes of faith, and a great terror to the merely religious (8:10–13).* When Jesus heard the centurion's analogy, 'he was astonished' (8:10). (Far better to astonish Jesus with our faith, as here, than with our unbelief, as in Mark 6:6.) What astonishes Jesus is the man's faith: 'I tell you the truth, I have not found anyone in Israel with such great faith' (8:10). Jesus' fellow Jews were steeped in the Scriptures, and their race had enjoyed centuries of covenantal relationship with God. Jesus seems to imply that, if anyone should identify him rightly and approach him with submissive faith it should be the Jew; but here is this Gentile, a centurion from the ranks of the Roman overlord, displaying faith of astonishing vigor and perception. It is possible, of course, that the man had read something of what we today call the Old Testament. But there is no record of Jesus having performed a miracle by word only and from a distance prior to this event (unless John 4:46ff. be judged a separate and earlier healing). Nevertheless the centurion by commenting on Jesus' authority has shown he has penetrated very near the heart of Jesus' identity; and so his faith is both a reflection of an attitude of heart that is right, and a christological confession of some depth. His faith is not only great, it is perceptive; or perhaps it is great because it is perceptive.

The centurion's remarkable faith won the healing of his servant. When Jesus says, 'Go! It will be done *just* as you believed it would' (8:13; emphasis added), he does not mean that the miracle performed was *in proportion* to the man's faith, nor even that the miracle was accomplished *because* of the man's faith (i.e., in a strong causal sense that would make faith not only the occasion but also the effective cause of the healing), but rather that the content of the miracle would be *what was expected* by the centurion's faith (similarly 15:28).

But there is more in store for the centurion and for others like him. Jesus insists that many will come from the east and the west (a way of referring to Gentile peoples), 'and will take their places at the feast with Abraham, Isaac and Jacob in the kingdom of heaven' (8:11). The picture is that of the messianic banquet, drawn from such Old Testament passages as Isaiah 25:6–9 (cf. 65:13–14) and considerably embellished in later Judaism. The banquet suggests a time of joy and celebration, the consummation of the kingdom; and Jesus here insists that many Gentiles will join in with the Jewish patriarchs on that great occasion. In the context, this can only be because they have responded with the centurion's faith to Jesus. The centurion saw in Jesus' authority the solution to his anguish, and approached him with the eyes of faith. In microcosm that is what men and women have been doing through the centuries: they perceive their need and recognize in Jesus the sole voice of authority that can meet their need, and they come to him in faith.

Not everyone recognizes Jesus' authority; others sense the power but do not respond with faith. Even some who naturally belong to the kingdom, that is, the Jews who had lived under the old covenant and had been the heirs of the promises, turn out to be rejected.

They too approach the great hall of the messianic banquet, lit up with a thousand lamps in joyous festivity; but they are refused admission, they are thrown outside into the blackness of night, 'where there will be weeping and gnashing of teeth' (8:12). The idea is not that there will be no Jews at the messianic banquet. After all, the patriarchs themselves are Jews, and all of Jesus' earliest followers were Jews. But Jesus insists that there is no automatic advantage to being a Jew. As he later says to those of his own race, 'Therefore I tell you that the kingdom of God will be taken away from you and given to a people who will produce its fruit' (21:43). An individual's faith, his or her response to the authority claims of Jesus, will prove decisive. The alternative to entrance into the kingdom is painted in horrible colors: literally *the* weeping and *the* gnashing of teeth, to emphasize the horror of the scene, the former suggesting suffering and the latter despair. The same authority of Jesus that proves such a great comfort to the eyes of faith now engenders terror in the merely religious.

This is not a teaching that is very acceptable to vast numbers in western Christendom today. It flies in the face of the great god Pluralism who holds much more of our allegiance than we are prone to admit. The test for religious validity in this environment is no longer truth but sincerity – as if sincerity were a virtue even when the beliefs underlying it are entirely mistaken. Teaching about hell is unpopular for another reason: it seems cruel to the modern mind, in which, unlike Scripture, it is popular and easy to believe in the love of God and difficult to make much sense of his holiness and wrath.

I must not stop and give this difficult subject the treatment it deserves; I hope to do so shortly in another publication. Nevertheless a few lines may not be out of place. Perhaps the most startling thing to observe is that Jesus

says far more about hell than anyone else in the Scripture.
If he speaks as the meek and humble teacher (Matt.
11:28–30), he also appears as the final judge (7:21–23) who
sends some to eternal punishment and others to eternal
life (25:31–46). It is impossible to accept a partial Jesus; for
one would be buying into a domesticated Jesus, one
shaped by our predilections, not one who can command
us or demand anything of us we are unprepared to give.
Second, from the few images of hell presented in the
Scripture, there is nothing to suggest that its residents
ever repent. Just as a great sinner who dies a lingering
and painful death may be consumed not by remorse but
by bitterness, so it is quite possible that hell continues on
and on because the rebellion of its citizens continues on
and on. Hell becomes a continuation of a life orientation
on this side: 'Let him who does wrong continue to do
wrong; let him who is vile con-tinue to be vile' (Rev.
22:11). And third, probably most of us entertain a thoroughly inadequate understanding of sin. The heart of sin
is not so much discrete acts of moral degradation, concrete steps of hardened rebellion, as an attitude of life that
is foundationally self-centered. That is the nature and
measure of our sin. Endemic to this horrible situation is
our utter inability to assess the matter rightly: how can
self-centeredness assess self-centeredness, except by criteria already utterly compromised? The only hope is for
God to speak to us from outside our selfishness. Once
grant that he has done so in Scripture and supremely in
Christ, and even our slowness to accept God's assessment
of our need and of our destiny apart from him becomes a
numbing judgment on our sinfulness.

In the immediate context, the alternatives – the messianic banquet or the darkness characterized by weeping
and gnashing of teeth – become starker precisely
because those assigned to each destiny are not drawn

from the polarities of what the world would judge to be moral behavior. Jesus does not set up a contrast between the ancient world's equivalent of Hitler and Francis of Assisi, or Idi Amin and Augustine, or Stalin and Mother Theresa. Those thrown outside are religious people, 'good' people, religiously privileged people. The only difference between them and those like the centurion who come from the east and the west to sit with the patriarchs at the messianic banquet is *faith* – the kind of faith displayed by the centurion, the faith that approaches Jesus in the posture of a supplicant and sees in him the sufficient answer to our need. Such revelation recognizes the unique authority of Jesus, and hungers above all that Jesus might use such authority to help us in ways we cannot help ourselves. Satisfied self-centeredness, even of a religious sort, is inimical to transforming faith. And that is why on the long haul the authority of Jesus will prove a great comfort to the eyes of faith, and a great terror to the merely religious.

This is the *kind* of faith we must exercise by God's help, when, on this side of the cross, we understand, even better than the centurion, the purpose of Jesus' coming, and sing:

> Not the labour of my hands
> Can fulfil thy law's demands;
> Could my zeal no respite know,
> Could my tears for ever flow,
> All for sin could not atone,
> Thou must save, and thou alone.
>
> Nothing in my hand I bring,
> Simply to thy cross I cling;
> Naked, come to thee for dress;
> Helpless, look to thee for grace;

Foul, I to the fountain fly;
Wash me, Saviour, or I die!

Augustus M. Toplady (1740–1778)

And that brings us to the final lesson to be learned about the nature of Jesus' authority as it is displayed in this passage.

5. The authority of Jesus is a function of his work on the cross (8:14–17). These first two healings (8:1–13) are capped by a brief account of the healing of Peter's mother-in-law (8:14–15), and a generalizing statement that lays to rest any suspicion that these were only occasional displays of power (8:16–17). Peter, of course, was married (cf. 1 Cor. 9:5); apparently his mother-in-law was living with Peter and his wife in Capernaum, the town which Jesus had also made his headquarters at this point (Matt. 4:13). The nature of the woman's illness is unclear: in those days the fever itself was viewed as a malady, not just a symptom. But Jesus healed her with a touch, even though Jewish tradition forbade touching persons with many kinds of fever. As in verse 3, Jesus' touch does not defile the healer but heals the defiled. The mother-in-law immediately got up and began to wait on Jesus: the point is made to attest the effectiveness and instantaneity of Jesus' healing power. He needs only to exercise his authority, and the deed is done.

But these healings are merely examples of a great host of healings and exorcisms he performed. On into the evening the needy came – a point that attests the pace of Jesus' ministry (although the parallels, Mark 1:32–34 and Luke 4:40–41, point out that the day was a Sabbath, and some may have wished to wait until sundown and the end of the Sabbath before venturing to carry their sick to Jesus, since carrying a burden was considered a forbidden act of work). He 'drove out the spirits with a word and healed all the sick' (Matt. 8:16). All this took place, we are told, to fulfil what was spoken through the prophet Isaiah: 'he took up our infirmities and carried our sorrows' (53:4).

This quotation is from the well-known passage of Scripture sometimes called the fourth Servant Song (Isa. 52:13 – 53:12). On the face of it, that passage seems to present the Servant as a sacrifice substituted that others might be spared: for example, 'But he was pierced for our transgressions, he was crushed for our iniquities; the punishment that brought us peace was upon him, and by his wounds we are healed' (53:5). In the New Testament this Servant Song is constantly linked to Jesus' death on the cross – not least by Matthew himself (20:28 [Isa. 53:10–12]; 27:12 [Isa. 53:7]; 27:57 [Isa. 53:9]; and elsewhere, e.g., Acts 8:32–33; 1 Peter 2:24). But here, apparently, Matthew is saying that Jesus' healing ministry, not his atoning death, is the way he 'took up our infirmities and carried our diseases.' This has prompted not a few scholars to suggest that Matthew here quotes Isaiah rather out of context.

In fact, the point of connection is profound. Both Scripture and Jewish tradition understood that all sickness is caused, directly or indirectly, by sin. When the direct connection is operative, a particular sin issues in a particular illness; and in that case healing of the illness cannot occur unless the sin is dealt with. But not every illness is the direct result of a specific sin. Sickness may reflect the fact that all of us live this side of the fall, under the curse, limited by mortality. Such sickness will plague us until the consummation of the kingdom, when there will be 'no more death or mourning or crying or pain' (Rev. 21:4), when the curse itself will have been overthrown (Rev. 22:3). In this larger sense, sickness is still connected with sin; but the connection is indirect, and finally remedied only by the return of Christ at the end of the age.

The New Testament recognizes both the direct and the indirect connections. In John 5, the man who had been paralyzed for thirty-eight years is told not to sin lest a worse thing befall him – which presupposes that the paralysis was the direct result of a specific sin. By contrast, in John 9, when the disciples ask Jesus whether the man born blind or his parents had sinned that he should be so afflicted, Jesus says neither option is correct: this situation came about for the glory of God. Outside the Gospels, some Christians in Corinth had fallen ill, and others had actually died, because of their improper approach to the Lord's Supper (1 Cor. 11:17–30). But in Galatians 4, Paul testifies that the reason he brought the gospel to his readers in the first instance was because of an illness: apparently when he arrived at the southern coast of what is now Turkey he contracted a fever, possibly malarial, and so headed north into the hills to escape the fetid atmosphere and to regain his health. There is no suggestion whatsoever that Paul was suffering on account of some specific sin in his life, still less that he was miraculously healed. Far from it: the illness was the Lord's providential means of bringing the gospel to the Galatians. The same Paul who on occasion performs healing miracles can on other occasions mention that he has had to leave Trophimus behind, ill; or that Timothy should take a little wine for his frequent infirmities.

Much more evidence could be gathered, but the heart of the matter can be summarized this way. First, all sickness is the result of the condition of sinfulness in which we find ourselves, but only some sickness is the direct result of immediate and specific sin. That perhaps suggests that illness ought to serve as an occasion for the

thoughtful person to engage in a little quiet self-exami-
nation. Second, whatever the immediate cause, some
sickness is healed in the Scripture, and some is not.
Modern voices that suggest God cannot or does not heal
miraculously today have little exegetical warrant to support their stance; but equally, those modern voices that
insist God inevitably grants healing provided only that
there is adequate faith have forfeited the balance of
Scripture and pursued a reductionism that once again
tries to domesticate God. The God who allows James to
be killed by Herod while providing escape for Peter is
the God who arranges for Paul to be ill while granting
Dorcas life.

Now we are in a better position to understand why
Matthew cites these lines from Isaiah. Matthew, after all,
understands that Jesus came to save his people from
their sin: he emphasizes that point in his first chapter
(1:21). The same authority that heals also forgives sin, as
Matthew emphasizes (9:1–8). And it is Jesus' death that
inaugurates the new covenant, which deals so effectively with sin (26:27–29). The ultimate undoing of sin
will result in the abolition of illness; in the consummated kingdom, as we have seen, there will be no more
suffering of any sort, but a bliss of righteousness and an
end to all suffering, savagery, and tears – as the prophets
themselves anticipated. When Isaiah 53 tells us that the
Servant bears our infirmities and carries our sicknesses,
it is the context of the Servant Song, as well as the understood connection between sin and suffering, that show
us that the way the Servant bears the sicknesses of
others is through his suffering and death, by which he
deals principally with both sin and suffering.

Granted, then, that the New Testament writers, including Matthew, understand Isaiah 53 in this way, why does
Matthew 8 draw the connection between Isaiah 53 and

Jesus' healing ministry? There can be only one reason. Matthew understands that Jesus' healing miracles were not simply acts of power, but were performed as a function of Jesus' atoning death still to take place. Because even within Jesus' ministry, before the cross, the kingdom was being inaugurated and demonstrated, it was appropriate that healings and exorcisms should be performed in anticipation of the great day when sickness and demonic power would be forever removed from God's people; but because all such benefits stem from Jesus' atoning death, those same healings can be understood to point beyond the authority of Jesus to the cross of Jesus. They are signs not only of Jesus' authority but also of his servanthood. As they are the anticipation of the consummated kingdom still awaited, so also are they the fruit of the cross-work of Jesus not yet performed. Matthew, writing *after* the death and resurrection of Jesus and therefore easily perceiving the connection, draws attention to it by citing Isaiah 53 in connection with Jesus' healing ministry. When Jesus healed Peter's mother-in-law, the centurion, the leper, and all the others, he did so not merely out of the abundance of power rightly his, but because he was to absorb in his own person, in his own act as a willing, atoning sacrifice, the sin bound up with suffering. Precisely because the healings were done in anticipation of Calvary, they fulfilled what was spoken through the prophet Isaiah: 'He took up our infirmities and carried our diseases.'

Two general conclusions must be drawn. First, it is important that Christians should not think of the benefits they have in Christ Jesus *apart from thinking about his atoning death*. When the structures of New Testament thought are put together, the death and resurrection of Jesus stand at the heart of everything else. The canonical Gospels move toward Jesus' death and resurrection; the apostles

and others in Acts preach in Jesus' death and resurrection
the remission of sins; the Epistles presuppose the atonement and build upon it. Even the blessed Holy Spirit,
given to us as the downpayment of the promised inheri-
tance, has been bequeathed to us in the wake of Jesus'
triumph on the cross and subsequent return to his Father.
*Jesus' powerful, transforming acts, whether in the days of his
flesh or today, must never be abstracted from his work on the
cross.* Nowhere, perhaps, is this truth more clearly enun-
ciated than in Colossians 1:15–20; but already it receives
subtle support in Matthew's Gospel.

Second, we must inevitably conclude (to use the modern jargon) that 'there is healing in the atonement.' But
this clause has been much abused. One party insists that,
because there is healing in the atonement, therefore
Christians must expect to be healed today. The atonement
has already provided this benefit, as it were; so if
Christians are not healed, it cannot be the fault of Jesus or
of his atonement, but of our unbelief. The opposing party,
struggling to avoid this unsettling conclusion, argues
therefore that there is no healing in the atonement: that is
something that is provided for only at the consummation.
But in fact, both sides have set the categories wrongly. The
truth of the matter is that there *is* healing in the atonement; but the atonement provides God's people with *all*
benefits that ultimately come to them. In that sense, there
is also a resurrection body in the atonement; but no one
uses that point to argue that all believers should today be
sporting resurrection bodies, and failure to do so betrays
a formidable lack of faith. The question is *not* whether or
not the atonement stands as the basis for all blessings that
come to God's children, but which of those benefits are
applied *now*, and which of them can be counted on *only
later*. Healing, judging by some of the passages already
briefly adduced, is one of those benefits that has been

secured by the cross, occasionally applied now, and promised for the new heaven and the new earth. If in God's mercy he grants healing now, whether by 'normal' or 'miraculous' means, we must be grateful; but we have no right to *claim* the benefit *now* simply because it has been secured by the work of Jesus on the cross.

In short, the authority of Jesus must never be seen in independence of his atoning sacrifice; it is always a function of his work on the cross. That simple truth ought to drive us back to basics again and again.

Conclusion

When Jesus confronts the world, his *authority* soon emerges as one of the crucial and most disputed storm centers. This is not an accidental result: if our sin is at root a defiance of God's authority, a deeply rooted self-centeredness at enmity with God and his claims, and in love with ephemeral dreams of autonomy, it cannot be surprising that when Jesus confronts the world his authority, the authority of God himself, soon erupts as one of the focal points of debate.

May all of us who read these pages pledge ourselves anew to submit joyfully to Jesus' authority, to come to him in full recognition that only he can meet our needs and sustain us both in this life and in the life to come, and give him thanks that all of his transforming power, whether exercised now or hereafter, stems from the immeasurably great sacrifice he underwent on our behalf.

Thine arm, O Lord, in days of old,
Was strong to heal and save;
It triumphed o'er disease and death,
O'er darkness and the grave.

To thee they went – the blind, the dumb,
The palsied, and the tame,
The leper with his tainted life,
The sick with fevered frame.

And, lo, thy touch brought life and health,
Gave speech, and strength, and sight;
And youth renewed and frenzy calmed
Owned thee, the Lord of light.
And now, O Lord, be near to bless,
As mighty as before,
In crowded street, by restless couch,
As by Gennesaret's shore.

Be thou our great Deliverer still,
Thou Lord of life and death;
Restore and quicken, soothe and bless,
With thine almighty breath;
To hands that work and eyes that see
Give wisdom's heavenly lore,
That whole and sick, and weak and strong,
May praise thee evermore.

Edward H. Plumptre (1821–1891)

2 (Matthew 8:18–34)

The Authentic Jesus

When Jesus saw the crowd around him, he gave orders to cross to the other side of the lake. Then a teacher of the law came to him and said, 'Teacher, I will follow you wherever you go.'

Jesus replied, 'Foxes have holes and birds of the air have nests, but the Son of Man has no place to lay his head.'

Another disciple said to him, 'Lord, first let me go and bury my father.'

But Jesus told him, 'Follow me, and let the dead bury their own dead.'

Then he got into the boat and his disciples followed him. Without warning, a furious storm came up on the lake, so that the waves swept over the boat. But Jesus was sleeping. The disciples went and woke him, saying, 'Lord, save us! We're going to drown!'

He replied, 'You of little faith, why are you so afraid?' Then he got up and rebuked the winds and the waves, and it was completely calm.

The men were amazed and asked, 'What kind of man is this? Even the winds and the waves obey him!'

When he arrived at the other side in the region of the Gadarenes, two demon-possessed men coming from the tombs met him. They were so violent that no one could pass that way. 'What do you want with us, Son of God?' they shouted. 'Have you come here to torture us before the appointed time?'

Some distance from them a large herd of pigs was feeding. The demons begged Jesus, 'If you drive us out, send us into the herd of pigs.'

He said to them, 'Go!' So they came out and went into the pigs, and the whole herd rushed down the steep bank into the lake and died in the water. Those tending the pigs ran off, went into the town and reported all this, including what had happened to the demon-possessed men. Then the whole town went out to meet Jesus. And when they saw him, they pleaded with him to leave their region.

Introduction

Very frequently our experience of something is different from our expectations. The experience itself may be far happier or far sadder than what we anticipated; but the difference between the two is marked.

For instance, we plan a family holiday with a detailed itinerary, and look forward to the two weeks with visceral enthusiasm. But if many of the planned excursions depend on fine weather, and if we endure two solid weeks of drizzle, our experience during those holidays will be radically different from our expectations. Someone may look forward to marriage with a dreamy-eyed, romantic perspective that believes marriage to be a universal panacea, the fulfillment of life's purposes and the ultimate solution to certain temptations. Marriage itself may then prove something of a disappointment: monumental quarrels can develop over the decision to squeeze or to roll the tube of toothpaste. Painful clashes recur until differing values and perspectives are resolved. Living at close quarters with another human being inevitably demands adjustments, give and take, forbearance, and a lot of hard work. Temptations do not seem much alleviated, merely refocused. On the other hand, it is also possible for someone to view marriage with a certain dread, based perhaps on painful memories of a shattered home, of a drunken and abusive father or a crabby and selfish mother; and then as the years roll by, one is suddenly struck by how peaceful this marriage has been, how rewarding, how fulfilling, how beneficial to both parties.

Christian work can also generate false expectations. A prospective missionary may anticipate the mission field with a romantic, even sentimental notion of service: standing under the shade of a palm tree, preaching powerfully to vast throngs of men and women who hang on your every word, counseling with profound biblical wisdom many national leaders who are overwhelmingly grateful for your leadership, building churches that are evangelistic and spiritually mature. Reality may prove disappointingly different. The missionary arrives in the designated country, and may find the food unpalatable and the flies prolific. The ordinary administrative details of life – shopping, going to the bank, securing a driver's license, repairing a puncture – take three or four times as much energy and time as at home. A year or two is devoted to gaining a still rudimentary knowledge of the new language. Nationals may have very mixed feelings about your presence; and the personality conflicts you faced at home are magnified under the stresses of an alien culture. You may be assigned for lengthy periods of time, not to preaching to great crowds, but to bookkeeping or running a school for missionary children. Alternatively, you may serve the Lord for years in a part of the world where there is very little fruit, and then suddenly and unpredictably enter a period of immense fruitfulness, tremendous joy, and almost breathless growth. Either way, expectations are shattered by reality.

When Jesus confronts the world, many of the world's expectations are destroyed. This was true during Jesus' earthly ministry. Many of his contemporaries were looking forward to a messiah who would turf out the Romans, raise the nation of Israel to supreme prominence in the international community, and introduce not only prosperity but a global centrality to Jerusalem such that foreigners would flock to her, bring tribute, and acknowledge that the God of the Jews was the true God. But not many focused much attention on the need for repentance, on the many promises of Scripture that anticipated thoroughgoing righteousness. And no one, so far as we know, clearly connected the promised messianic king with the promised suffering servant, and understood that one person would take up both strands in himself. Even Jesus' closest disciples failed to make these connections until after the resurrection. The world's expectations turned out to be too narrow, too partisan, too limited, and sometimes just plain wrong. The authentic Jesus outstripped the expectations.

When Jesus confronts the world today, similar misconceptions must often be cleared away. When an individual first begins to draw near to Jesus, he or she often carries along an assortment of expectations urgently in need of modification. Perhaps the would-be convert thinks that Jesus is a spiritual 'fix' worth trying, a fine source of spiritual fulfilment – without raising questions about sin, truth, obedience, or the like. In some communities, family or cultural pressures teach that profession of faith in Jesus is a step to local acceptability, always provided, of course, that religion is not taken too seriously. When someone from that sort of background first reads the Bible with real understanding, and finds out what the authentic Jesus is like, it can produce something of a jolt.

In this series, we have seen that one of the points of friction that develops when Jesus confronts the world is the sheer authority of Jesus (chap. 1). That theme of Jesus authority continues in the verses now before us. Whoever dares make allegiance to family secondary to allegiance to him (8:22) is either a lunatic or someone with authority nothing less than divine; for only to God could such supreme loyalty be rightly due. In the next paragraph, Jesus demonstrates his authority over the forces of nature (8:23–27); and in the final section of Matthew 8, not only does he display his power over the world of demons, but also the demons recognize both his right and his power to do so, especially 'at the appointed time' (8:29 – presumably the end of the age).

But I shall not pursue the theme of authority in this chapter. Instead, I shall cast the confrontation between Jesus and the world in wider terms, to show that the authentic Jesus, the real Jesus, regularly turns out to be unforeseen, unpredictable, unnegotiable, and (in any real encounter with him) unavoidable. I do not mean to suggest that everyone finds him unavoidable: in this life, that is demonstrably untrue, for many do not even hear of him. But where there is a genuine encounter between Jesus and an individual or a group of people, when Jesus does in fact confront the world, then who and what the authentic Jesus really is becomes unavoidable.

What, then, are some of the characteristics of the real Jesus that are often overlooked? From these verses we may observe four of them.

Some Characteristics of the Authentic Jesus

1. The authentic Jesus makes demands that are personal and costly (8:18–22). Two people are introduced in this pair of vignettes – a teacher of the law (8:18–20), traditionally called a scribe, and another man, simply designated a disciple (8:21–22). Some see a contrast between the two: scribes are always opponents of Jesus, and so this one is simply put off, whereas the disciple is told to follow Jesus.

In fact, this interpretation is artificial. Jesus does not have *categories* of opponents (e.g., 'All scribes are enemies of Jesus'); rather, he assesses men and women as they divide around him. The 'teacher of the law' category can be applied to *Christian* teachers (13:52; 23:34; the same word in Greek). This one in 8:19 approaches Jesus respectfully: even though scribes were first and foremost teachers themselves, he addresses Jesus as 'teacher,' and there is nothing in the context to suggest his approach is any thing but sincere. The opening words of verse 21, 'another of his disciples,' mean that Matthew viewed the teacher of the law as a disciple and the second man who is mentioned as 'another of his disciples.' After all, the term *disciple* does not mean, despite arguments to the contrary, that a firmly committed 'Christian' is in view. Applied to the ministry of Jesus, it customarily refers to a broad spectrum of people who are at that point following Jesus. That following can be quite physical: after all Jesus was an itinerant preacher, and some folk followed him from place to place in order to glean more from his teaching and become one of his intimates. Similarly John the Baptist had 'disciples' (Matt. 11:2) who followed him. Such followers, such disciples, were more likely to be sincerely pursuing Jesus' teaching than at least some others who would not or could not find the time to do so; but their number also included Judas Iscariot. Thus both the men in Matthew 8:18–22 are disciples of some sort. If Jesus uses the words *follow me* only to the second, it is not because only he is a true disciple, but because only he is planning *not* to follow Jesus at that point, and needs to be told to reverse his commitments.

The basic point of these verses is simple enough. Two disciples (in the sense I have just explained) promise some kind of allegiance to Jesus, and in some measure Jesus rebuffs them both. But there is a difference between the two. The first is too quick in promising; the second is too slow in performing.

At first glance the words of the first seem promising: 'Teacher, I will follow you wherever you go.' We might be reminded of the unconditional promise of Ittai to David when the king, facing a revolt, counseled him to change his allegiance. Ittai responds, 'As surely as the LORD lives, and as my lord the king lives, wherever my lord the king may be, whether it means life or death, there will your servant be' (2 Sam. 15:21). We might also think of the peerless determination of Ruth when Naomi tries to dissuade Ruth from following her: 'Don't urge me to leave you or to turn back from you. Where you go I will go, and where you stay I will stay. Your people will be my people and your God my God. Where you die I will die, and there I will be buried. May the LORD deal with me, be it ever so severely, if anything but death separates you and me' (Ruth 1:16–17). But Jesus detects in this man less the commitment of an Ittai and a Ruth than the overconfidence of a Peter, who would later boldly promise, 'Even if all fall away on account of you, I never will . . . Even if I have to die with you, I will never disown you' (Matt. 26:33,35) – only to disown his master shamefully, even with oaths.

Jesus' reply tests the scribe's commitment, but probably reveals what Jesus diagnosed his problem to be. 'Foxes have holes and birds of the air have nests,' Jesus responds, 'but the Son of Man has no place to lay his head' (8:20). This response stresses not so much Jesus' poverty as his homelessness. Apparently he detected that the teacher of the law envisaged a connection with Jesus that would secure stability, perhaps even privilege. After all, if Jesus is the Messiah (he may well have thought), and if the Messiah is to rule in a powerful and wealthy kingdom supremely blessed by God, then it would be wise to become a close follower of Jesus now, in order to get on the inside track when the day of glory dawns. Alternatively, his motives may not have been so crass. Perhaps he liked much of what he saw and heard in Jesus, and decided to follow him more closely, but without giving much thought to the kind of itinerant ministry Jesus was actually exercising, and to the difficulties and privations such work entailed.

Whatever the case, the hurdle Jesus erects for the man establishes an important point. As one commentator puts it, 'Nothing was less aimed at by our Lord than to have *followers*, unless they were genuine and sound; he is as far from desiring this as it would have been easy to obtain it.' Little has done more to harm the witness of the Christian church than the practice of filling its ranks with every volunteer who is willing to make a little profession, talk fluently of experience, but display little of perseverance. Too often the old maxim proves true: Soon ripe, soon rotten. This is not to deny that conversion may take place quickly, nor is it to suggest that early profession of allegiance to Christ is invariably spurious. Rather, it is to insist that part of a genuine closing with Christ at some point entails counting the cost, and coming to grips with the fact that loyalty to Jesus brings with it demands that may be costly.

The second man, another of Jesus' disciples, utters a request which, on the surface of things, seems reasonable: 'Lord, first let me go and bury my father' (8:21). Commentators have wavered between two opinions: either the man was asking for the time needed to bury and mourn for his father, recently deceased; or else his father was aged, and the man was waiting for him to die and be buried before he would consider following Jesus more closely. Either way, this man was reflecting Jewish Palestinian piety: sons were expected to look after their parents, and to bury them when the time came.

Jesus' answer is stunning: 'Follow me, and let the dead bury their own dead' (8:22). The utterance is, of course, paradoxical: 'Let the (spiritually) dead bury the (physically) dead'; but it is no less biting for that. It cannot mean that Jesus is encouraging chronic disrespect for parents, when elsewhere he can berate those who used the temple contribution system to withhold from their parents the support that was their due. Nowhere does the New Testament set aside the emphasis of Deuteronomy 27:14,16: 'The Levites shall recite to all the people of Israel in a loud voice: . . . "Cursed is the man who dishonours his father or his mother." Then all the people shall say, "Amen!"'

In fact, this is a powerful way of getting at the point Jesus will later make explicit: 'Anyone who loves his father or mother more than me is not worthy of me; anyone who loves his son or daughter more than me is not worthy of me; and anyone who does not take his cross and follow me is not worthy of me. Whoever finds his life will lose it, and whoever loses his life for my sake will find it' (Matt. 10:37–39). Jesus' concern in 8:22 is not so much to forbid all who would follow him from attending the funerals of near relatives, as it is to expose the danger of merely qualified discipleship. Indeed, sometimes Jesus purposely uses language that is rather shocking, not because it is meant to be taken literally, but because it most tellingly makes the point. For example, in Matthew 5:27–30 Jesus insists that the eye that lusts is best plucked out; the hand that touches what is forbidden is best cut off. One of the early church fathers took this literally, and castrated himself; but in one sense even self-castration is simply not radical enough. Jesus' point is not that self-mutilation is an effective way to deal with sin, but that sin must be dealt with radically, at its root, even if such dealings are costly. Similarly in Matthew 8, the point is not so much that people should not be concerned for their parents, but that if concern for parents becomes an excuse for not following Jesus, or for delay in following Jesus, then concern for parents, as important as it is, is being too highly valued.

Some who read these lines have made difficult and costly decisions regarding their families. A colleague from a wealthy family was disinherited when he went into the ministry. A close friend, when she became a Christian, was bombarded by emotional barrages from her unbelieving family: 'Don't you think we are good enough? Didn't we bring you up right? Are you now saying that you are better than we?' Indeed, the division can become more acute as the months pass, and the new convert recognizes that his or her goals and values are in certain respects no longer in line with those inherited from the family.

The two vignettes in these verses, then, teach us that the authentic Jesus makes demands that are often personal and costly. That is why Jesus can elsewhere tell parables the point of which is that would-be disciples *ought* to count the cost before they promise too much (Luke 14:25–35).

Certainly Paul understood that following Jesus entailed costly decisions. They may not be the same for every Christian; but for him they involved shame, pain, suffering, privation, and large-scale rejection (1 Cor. 4:8–13; 2 Cor. 11:21–33) – even being considered 'the scum of the earth, the refuse of the world.'

This point is frequently misunderstood by evangelicals, precisely because we have (rightly) stressed the importance of justification by grace, the freedom of God in giving salvation. Our works do not save us; we can be acquitted before the bar of God's justice and declared righteous in his presence solely on the basis of God's grace given us in Christ Jesus. But does that mean there is no cost for us to consider at all?

The kind of misapprehension that frequently occurs cropped up recently when a friend of mine was witnessing to a lady of the Jehovah's Witnesses persuasion. She asked, rather suspiciously, what he thought the way of salvation was; and he replied with a more or less traditional evangelical presentation, stressing the grace of God. She replied with words to this effect: 'That's what I thought you would say. But I couldn't bear a religion that costs me nothing.'

Her misunderstanding was profound; in fact, her response betrayed a double misunderstanding. She needed to come to grips with the fact that in the Scripture salvation turns on God's free gift. In that sense she could contribute nothing but her sin; and if that is the kind of religion she could not stand, she was rejecting the biblical revelation. So in the first place, she misunderstood the nature of salvation in the Scripture. But on the other hand, those elementary truths do not mean that there are no costs at all, no personal demands. Biblical salvation is paid for by someone else: in that sense it is free. But individual appropriation of it entails repentance, personal death to self-interest, principal submission to the lordship of Jesus Christ. These are not meritorious acts. They are, finally, evidence of the grace of God in the Christian life, but they are no less personal or costly for that. So she displayed a second misunderstanding: she failed to see that salvation that has been paid for, and is therefore free, nevertheless works in our lives so powerfully that it transforms us, confronts our will, demands our devotion and allegiance, and calls forth our deepest commitment.

In concrete terms, the 'costs' Christians pay in the west, as compared with those paid by many Christians in the world, are very small. Principally, however, they are exactly the same for all Christians: death to self-interest, a daily 'dying' that can be quite painful. But it is precisely that attitude that breeds a Borden of Yale, who abandoned great wealth and status to prepare for ministry in the Middle East. Only a short time after his arrival, he contracted the disease that killed him; and as he lay dying, with others bemoaning the 'waste,' his conclusion was firm: 'No reserve; no retreat; no regrets.' In one sense, our salvation costs us absolutely nothing; in another, it costs us not less than everything. The former is true because Jesus paid it all; the latter is possible because Jesus enables us to respond to his upward call. Those who stress the latter and neglect the former may never learn that salvation is by grace alone; those who stress the former and neglect the latter may buy into a cheap facsimile of grace that knows little of the biblical gospel and less of biblical holiness.

The authentic Jesus makes demands that are personal and costly.

2. *The authentic Jesus is far more wonderful than even his most intimate followers suspect (8:23–27).* Over the centuries some pretty fantastic interpretations of this miracle have been advanced. Tertullian argued that the boat

stands for the church: those who are in the church with Jesus can weather any storm, for he will protect them. That old interpretation has been dressed up again in modern garb: this section betrays the dangers facing Matthew's church, and the point is that as the disciples who *followed* him into the boat were safe, so those who *follow* Jesus in true discipleship are safe.

But this will not do. The verb *to follow* is not a technical one that invariably refers to true discipleship. It can be used to describe the action of the crowd, not the disciples (Matt. 4:25; 8:1,10; 12:15); indeed, in 9:19 Jesus and his disciples *follow* the ruler (the same verb in Greek) to his home – which certainly does not mean that Jesus had become a genuine disciple of the ruler! The point of the account is not so much focused on the nature of discipleship as on the person of Christ: it ends with the ejaculation, 'What kind of man is this? Even the winds and the waves obey him!' (8:27).

Sudden, violent squalls are not uncommon on Galilee, which lies six hundred feet below sea level. Hot, steamy air can start to rise, drawing in a rush of air from the desert that churns the surface of the lake into a violent cauldron. Here men cry out in alarm; and Jesus (as one commentator rather quaintly puts it) 'does not chide them for disturbing him with their prayers, but for disturbing themselves with their fears.' 'You of little faith,' he cries, 'why are you so afraid?'

The words *little faith* may not so much refer to quantity of faith as to its impoverished nature (as in 17:20, where faith like the grain of a mustard seed is not *large* faith but a certain *kind* of faith). Jesus presupposes that proper faith would drive out fear; he rebukes the disciples in that in their case fear has driven out faith. Clearly they have enough faith to turn to him for help; but the desperation of their cry and their astonished remarks after the miracle show their faith is not very mature. Their attitude is something like that of a crowd toward an illusionist, a modern magician: they believe he is going to do something remarkable, but gasp in surprise when it is done. In the case of the disciples, the situation is heightened by the danger of their situation (which does not of course apply to the crowd watching a magician).

Modern Christians will sympathize with the disciples a little when we remember our own prayers. We sometimes fall into difficult straits, and cry to God for help. Our credal stance is that God is a prayer-hearing and prayer-answering God; we believe he can resolve the difficulty both for his glory and for our good. But such is the poor quality of our faith that in many instances when God has answered, often in ways vastly superior to what we expected, we are greatly surprised. It is then that we lift our voices with renewed understanding:

> Sometimes a light surprises
> The Christian while he sings;
> It is the Lord who rises
> With healing in his wings.
> When comforts are declining,
> He grants the soul again
> A season of clear shining,
> To cheer it after rain.
>
> In holy contemplation,
> We sweetly then pursue
> The theme of God's salvation,
> And find it ever new:
> Set free from present sorrow,
> We cheerfully can say,
> E'en let the unknown morrow
> Bring with it what it may.

It can bring with it nothing
But he will bear us through;
Who gives the lilies clothing
Will clothe his people too;
Beneath the spreading heavens,
No creature but is fed;
And he who feeds the ravens
Will give his children bread.

Though vine nor fig-tree neither
Their wonted fruit should bear,
Though all the field should wither,
Nor flocks nor herds be there,
Yet, God the same abiding,
His praise shall tune my voice;
For, while in him confiding,
I cannot but rejoice.

William Cowper (1731–1800)

But the most serious deficiency of faith displayed by the disciples lay in their failure to recognize who Jesus really is. If they had truly come to terms with the kind of messiah Jesus was, could they really have thought that a squall on Galilee could swamp the boat and take the life of the heaven-sent Redeemer whose mission was to die in shame and rise in triumph for the salvation of his people? Could a storm snuff out the life of him who is the agent of creation? That is the point Matthew is making when he records the final exclamations of the disciples: they have not come to grips yet with who he is; and that is precisely why their faith is so beggarly.

The lesson is well put in a song by Mary A. Baker that I remember my mother singing, a song no longer well known in the church. It pictures the disciples crying out:

Master, the tempest is raging;
The billows are tossing high!
The sky is o'ershadowed with blackness,
No shelter or help is nigh!
Carest thou not that we perish?
How canst thou He asleep,
When each moment so madly is threat'ning
A grave in the angry deep?

To which Jesus replies:

The winds and the waves shall obey my will:
Peace! Be still!
Whether the wrath of the storm-tossed sea,
Or demons, or men, or whatever it be,
No water can swallow the ship where lies
The Master of ocean, and earth, and skies.
They all shall sweetly obey my will:
Peace! Be still! Peace! Be still!
They all shall sweetly obey my will:
Peace. Peace. Be still.

Jesus is always better than our fears. Moreover, our faith will be most stable *if we center it on who Jesus is.* Faith urgently needs to know, not so much what Jesus will do or what promises he may have made that are applicable to this or that situation, but *who Jesus is.* The Christian must learn that knowing the authentic Jesus better is what strengthens faith the most. We discover with increasing delight that Jesus is always far more wonderful than we had anticipated.

Indeed, all three of the portions that constitute the section of Matthew we are studying in this chapter (8:18–34) include some paradoxical aspects of Christ's nature. In the first, Jesus says that *the Son of Man* has no

place to lay his head (8:20). The expression was ambiguous in Jesus' day. It could be used as a simple self-reference; it was sometimes associated with the sufferings of
the Messiah; but it could also signal the glories of the
Messiah, in direct allusion to Daniel 7:13–14, where one
like a son of man receives a kingdom from God himself,
the Ancient of Days (cf. Matt. 26:64). Here in 8:20, there
is a simple self-reference, with overtones of privation
('no place to lay his head'); but Christians after the resurrection would not be able to avoid the connection with
Daniel 7, and marvel that in Jesus there was combined
kingly authority and the heart of a servant. In the second
paragraph, Jesus is asleep in the boat, exhausted from
the exertions of his ministry; yet he remains Lord of
nature, muzzling the storm by his word, exercising the
authority of God himself who controls and stills the seas
(Job 38:8–11; Ps. 29:3–4,10–11; 65:5–7; 89:9; 107:23–32). In
the third, he is recognized even by the demons as the
one who has final authority on the day of judgment; but
the Gadarenes implore him to leave their territory, and
he quietly leaves without exercising any judgment at all.

But these paradoxical features in Christ's nature are
the very things that give us such confidence in him. He
knew by experience the loneliness of homelessness, the
sleep of exhaustion, and the rejection of thoughtless
people; yet he was the glorious Son, the Lord of nature,
the Judge of all in earth and heaven. Small wonder the
writer of the Epistle to the Hebrews delights to remember that our champion has been touched with the feelings of our infirmities; but because he is the Lord, he has
the capacity to provide all the succor we need. This is the
authentic Jesus.

3. *The authentic Jesus puts spiritual and human realities before
other considerations (8:28–34). Some wag has suggested that*

*when the disciples as*ked what kind of man Jesus was (8:27), the demons went out to tell them (8:28–29). That may have been the result; but it was certainly not the demons' intention, and it is doubtful that the disciples saw it that way at the time.

Nevertheless, although the passage is not particularly aimed at giving us a detailed knowledge of demons, it may be worth reflecting a little on what it does suggest about them. In the western world, there are still many who prefer to demythologize demons: demons, they say, are not real, spiritual beings but popular projections of evil. Only the inroads of philosophical materialism could read that conclusion into the New Testament evidence; only those completely ignorant of spiritual warfare, not only in parts of the world under the influence of animism but now also increasingly in occult centers in the west, could voice such skepticism with so much confidence and condescension.

In the account before us, the demons are able to dissociate themselves from the men they possess (8:32). They recognize Jesus; in that sense they know him better than the disciples do. They know that Jesus is the unique Son of God; yet they are demons still. As one writer puts it, 'He is the firstborn of hell, that knows Christ, and yet hates him, and will not be subject to his law.' They are even aware of their ultimate fate (cf. Jude 6; Rev. 20:10), and that Jesus is the one who will consign them to it; but that knowledge in their case breeds taunts, violence, and hatred, not repentance. What distinguishes saints from demons is loving obedience, not naked knowledge.

These demons can animate other beings than humans. Why they should beg to be sent into the herd of pigs (Mark 5:13 says there were about two thousand animals) is not self-evident. Some have suggested that demons like to clothe themselves in bodies; but if so, why should their first action after being dismissed to the swine be the destruction of their new home? More likely, their hatred of the Creator extends to his creation. Whatever will do damage, especially against people (as in the destruction of herds people own), will be desirable to them.

But one of the points of the story is that Jesus has matchless, unassailable authority over *all* powers of darkness and evil spirits. Later on, the disciples would be stymied by a case of demon possession with which they tried to deal (Matt. 17:14–20); but Jesus is never so limited. The present incident takes place in the Decapolis area, largely inhabited by Gentiles; and the herd of pigs, which no self-respecting Jew would keep or tend, equally betrays the Gentile cast of the context. But Jesus is not limited in his authority to a Jewish environment. He is not bound by geography or race, who commends the Gentile centurion, who can leash the forces of nature, who can multiply five loaves and two small fishes, who can heal the sick and raise the dead, and who can turn sinners into saints.

But the account does not end with reflection on Jesus' authority. After Jesus' miracle, those tending the pigs run off and tell the town folk what had happened – 'including what had happened to the demon-possessed men' (8:33). The news was startling: a large herd of swine had been destroyed, and with it the wealth and livelihood of many people; and two demoniacs, well-known and universally avoided as dangerous, were now restored. So the whole town goes out to meet Jesus; but instead of focusing on the marvelous transformation of the two men who had been possessed, instead of asking further if Jesus might help others in their number, they apparently focus on their fiscal losses, and plead with him to leave their region (8:34).

Some human beings prefer pigs to people. People are fine – but not if they adversely affect my pocketbook. Why Jesus allowed the demons to possess and destroy the pigs is not clear. At one level their loss becomes part of the entire sweep of disasters, illnesses, storms, sorrows, and death that are part of the human condition this side of the new heaven and the new earth. Why Jesus granted the demons their request when he could have done something else is merely one of a thousand similar questions: Why did he not stop the injustices of Rome? Why did he heal only the one paralytic by the pool (John 5), and not all who were present? Why were not more raised from the dead? This kind of question I do not propose to address here;[2] but whatever answers we give, it is clear that the least that must be said of this account is that Jesus puts spiritual and human realities above other considerations. The release of the two men who had been demon-possessed is clearly of more importance to him than the loss of the two thousand pigs; the limitation of demonic activity is of greater moment than fiscal considerations.

This is of a piece with many biblical emphases. It is easy for us to devote much of our thought and energy to matters that, in the light of eternity, are of *relative* unimportance. Politics/sport, entertainment, the daily administration of family matters, clothes, health, education, and the like all enjoy varying degrees of importance; but compared with the really basic questions these subjects fade into insignificance – or, more accurately, these subjects find their true significance *only when they are seen as subsets of the really fundamental concerns*. Such concerns include righteousness, knowing God savingly both now and for all eternity, growing in thoughtful obedience to Jesus Christ, freedom from sin and from demonic power, displaying the love of Christ in lives transformed by the Spirit he has bequeathed.

The priorities we set, consciously or unconsciously, betray what we judge to be important. This question is raised in many different ways in the Bible. One of the most intriguing is found in 1 Corinthians 7, where Paul is talking about marriage, divorce, and related matters. After discussing various combinations of problems, his line of thought takes an important turn:

> Now about virgins: I have no command from the Lord, but I give a judgment as one who by the Lord's mercy is trustworthy. *Because of the present crisis* [emphasis added], I think that it is good for you to remain as you are. Are you married? Do not seek a divorce. Are you unmarried? Do not look for a wife. But if you do marry, you have not sinned; and if a virgin marries, she has not sinned. But those who marry will face many troubles in this life, and I want to spare you this.
>
> What I mean, brothers, is that the time is short. From now on those who have wives should live as if they had none; those who mourn, as if they did not; those who are happy, as if they were not; those who buy something, as if it were not theirs to keep; those who use the things of the world, as if not engrossed in them. For this world in its present form is passing away. (7:25–31)

These verses are often misunderstood in one of two ways. Some understand the words *the present crisis* to refer to a bout of persecution. Because of this crisis, it is argued, it might be best for Christians contemplating marriage to put the idea on hold. Oppressive forces can apply horrible pressure by making family members the targets of their attacks. Living singly may then provide the best opportunity for serving Christ without compromise or distraction. But this interpretation really will not do. There is not a shred of evidence that the Corinthian church was undergoing persecution at that point in its history; indeed, a strong whiff of persecution might have done it a great deal of good. Besides, this interpretation does not really explain verses 30–31: what exactly is the connection between this alleged persecution and mourning or being happy? And is Paul in verse 29 really advocating celibacy for married folk, when in the opening verses of the chapter he has so strongly insisted that partners in marriage must *not* abandon sexual activity, except under very restrictive conditions?

The second false interpretation argues that 'the present crisis' refers to Paul's belief that the Lord Jesus was going to come so soon, within a few years at most, that the Corinthian Christians should live their life in the light of that impending event. I am not persuaded, on broader grounds, that this is a fair interpretation of Paul; and in any case it leaves us with the unavoidable conclusion that Paul was wrong, since almost two thousand years have elapsed without the Saviour's return.

What Paul is referring to by his words *the present crisis* is the entire period between the first advent of Christ and the second. This entire age is characterized by crisis, however long or short it may be. During this period, called 'the last hour' by John (1 John 2:18), this world in its present form is passing away (1 Cor. 7:31). The emphasis is not on the *shortness* of the time left for this world, but on the *transitoriness* of this world. During this period between the advents, Christians must learn to live 'as if not': *everything* linked exclusively to an age that is passing must fall under the judgment of God's 'as if not.' Christians are so linked with the age to come, they so live with eternity's values in view, that the joys and sorrows and realities that are part of this age cannot

be allowed to dominate their lives. Marriage is important here; but in the new heaven and the new earth, there
is neither marriage nor giving in marriage. The wise
Christian will learn to view marriage 'as if not' – that is,
marriage will no longer be a dominating category, but
viewed from the eternal perspective. Within this framework, marriage is still perfectly acceptable (7:28); but it
can no longer be viewed as the goal of life, the promise
of perfect bliss, the fulfillment of all human aspirations.
The same is true of *whatever* makes the children of this
world happy, or mourn; it is true of *everything* that is
bought and sold. All is placed under God's 'as if not':
Christians live with the perspectives of the new age so
deeply embedded in their minds and hearts that the foci
of this age are held more loosely, '*as if* they do *not*' have
permanent validity or ultimate importance – precisely
because *they do not!*

In short, just as the authentic Jesus puts spiritual and
human realities before other considerations, his followers must do the same. We may rejoice in all that God
gives us here, so richly to enjoy; but we must never con-
fuse the blessings he gives us that are irretrievably
linked to this passing age with the blessings he gives us
that will last for all eternity.

*4. The authentic Jesus consistently overturns many common
expectations.* This point emerges not from a particular
verse or section in the chapter before us, but from the
flow of the argument both in this chapter and throughout the Gospels. One of the most self-evident aspects of
Jesus' ministry is its flexibility. Here is someone who
has exactly the *right* word for the harlot, the tax collector, the priest, the teacher of the law, the common lab-
orer, the would-be disciple, the Pharisee, the crowds of
common folk, the smooth-tongued interrogator, the

Roman official, the soldier, the grieving sister, the blind, the poor.

But there is more than mere flexibility here. Any polished person, skilled in public relations, can make small talk with all and sundry. Jesus' flexibility is not characterized by gifted small talk. In every recorded conversation he gets to the heart of the other's being. Exposed to view are the needs, values, selfishness, weakness, hurts, or pride that chiefly characterize the individual now being addressed.

In addition to the insight displayed by Jesus in this chapter, we might briefly mention a number of other instances. When a well-instructed Pharisee by the name of Nicodemus respectfully but hesitantly approaches, Jesus immediately turns to Nicodemus's area of expertise: the Scriptures. Nicodemus is apparently probing Jesus to find out if he is the Messiah; but Jesus' response drives Nicodemus, himself 'Israel's teacher' (John 3:10), to reflect on Old Testament promises that under the new covenant there would be clean, Spirit-renewed hearts – what Jesus calls a 'new birth.' To the rich young ruler whose god was his wealth, Jesus prescribes that he give away his possessions (Matt. 19:16–30). To the disciples who were jockeying for position (Matt. 18), Jesus makes appeal to a child as the standard of what proper response is like in the kingdom. And to religious leaders more concerned to trap Jesus in his words and to tear down his ministry than to bow before him and acknowledge him as Lord, Jesus not only responds with sharp replies on a case-by-case basis (Matt. 22), but also delivers a blistering yet grieving denunciation (Matt. 23). To Zacchaeus (Luke 19), Jesus' presence and personal interest seem to have been enough to bring about restitution.

One interesting dimension about all this diversity is what Jesus does not say in each of these instances. He may tell the rich young ruler to sell all he has; he does *not* lay down this requirement to Nicodemus, nor to the disciples, nor even to Zacchaeus. The 'new birth' predicted under the new covenant stands as part of the Old Testament Scriptures; but only Nicodemus is berated for not having grasped it. The model of a child's responsiveness and simple faith is not applied by Jesus to Zacchaeus, Nicodemus, or the rich young ruler.

What, then, is the commonality in all of this, other than Jesus' flexibility and peerless skills in spiritual diagnosis? The answer comes clear in the wake of two reflections. First, the gospel of Jesus Christ is a massive structure that can be applied to tremendously diverse circumstances. Second, it is wisely applied in most cases in ways that stand *directly opposite* to the circumstances of the individual.

To take a couple of unambiguous instances: Paul writes, 'For he who was a slave when he was called by the Lord is the Lord's freedman; similarly, he who was a free man when he was called is Christ's slave' (1 Cor. 7:22); and James insists, 'The brother in humble circumstances ought to take pride in his high position. But the one who is rich should take pride in his low position, because he will pass away like a wild flower' (Jam. 1:9–10). The damage that could be done if these points are applied in inverse array is incalculable. If the slave is told again and again that as a Christian he is still a slave, and nothing more, while the free man is told that the gospel of Christ is a liberating thing, and he is privileged to share in the rich heritage of Christ, the declarations, though true, are at best serious misapplications of the gospel, and at worst morally and spiritually catastrophic. The slave may indeed have to be told that conversion does not necessarily bring with it an automatic change in his physical position; but he must also be told that in the light of Christ's

cross-work, and in the light of the prospect of Christ's
return, his status before God (which on the long haul is
what counts) is immensely different from what it was.
Slave he may be; but he is now a child of God, an heir of
God and a joint heir with Jesus Christ. Meanwhile the free
man may need to have some of his arrogance before the
slaves curtailed; and in that sense he is wise to think of
himself as a fellow slave – a slave of Jesus Christ. Similar
sensitivity must be shown in the application of the gospel
to the rich and to the poor, as James shows.

In other words, the gospel is not only big enough to be
applicable to highly diverse circumstances, but also is
most fittingly applied in ways that fly in the face of the
individual involved. The reason is not hard to find. The
complex diversity of the human condition has at its core
a handful of rudimentary commonalities. Among these
is our sinfulness. Apart from grace, we rebel against God
in some fashion – whether in social rebellion, religious
perversion, moral delinquency, sheer arrogance, aped
humility, or some other form. When Jesus confronts the
world, he confronts sinners. Some are crushed, profoundly aware of their guilt, hungry for the forgiving
word. Others are oppressed, guilty no doubt, but also
discouraged, defeated, and eager to hear the reassurance
that there is justice in the universe and that we may live
with a longer-range vision than the contemporary political or economic climate permits. Still others are so full
of themselves and their accomplishments, so little aware
of the favor that has been shown them in the circumstances of their birth, upbringing, education, and material advantages that the only religion they want is a
domesticated variety; but what they need is rebuke, the
sharp exposure of their danger and real need.

Among those who read these words will be persons of
good birth and high breeding; there will also be some

who do not know who their fathers are, and who spent much of their lives in foster homes. Some will be quite wealthy; others could not possibly afford the price of this book, and are reading it only because they managed to borrow a copy from a friend or a library. Some will have been reared in Christian homes, and may not even be sure of the date of their conversion; others will have been skid-row alcoholics or drug addicts who were converted and marvelously and publicly transformed. It is important for all of us who are Christians, regardless of our backgrounds, to recognize that although the gospel applies to us, the particular elements that must be *stressed* in each case, the particular elements that we must apply to ourselves most strenuously, are precisely those elements most at variance with our position.

In short, the gospel can be applied with such flexibility precisely because the needs turn out to have more commonalities behind them than a casual glance might suggest. That is also the reason why Jesus consistently overturns so many common expectations. Our expectations are inevitably bound up with who we are; who we are is bound up with our ignorance of and rebellion against God. Despite our diversity, that is what Jesus and his ministry inevitably confront. Small wonder then that Jesus overthrows our categories and our expectations; for if he did not, he could not possibly be the one who was sent to save his people from their sins (Matt. 1:21).

The same truth has a bearing on modern discussions about contextualization – the need for the gospel to be shaped in large part by the culture in which it is being promulgated. In large part, the insights from recent treatments of contextualization are valid and important. Indeed, that is why John's Gospel does not sound exactly the same as Luke's: not only was John a different writer, but also he was ministering to a different audience, with different needs and categories. But the point can be pushed too far. Although the gospel must be presented to any group in terms of the categories and felt needs of that group, just as Paul wisely shapes his presentation of the gospel to the Athenians to take into account their intellectual history and structures (Acts 17), *it must always press on to the point where it is in some measure subverting and overthrowing the categories of that culture*. It must do so because all cultures are in some degree and particulars in rebellion against God, and will be judged by him. If the presentation of the gospel remains entirely congenial to any culture, it can only be because the gospel has been eviscerated, stripped of its stark independence – hopelessly tamed, like a pet poodle, to do the bidding of that culture.

Examples are not hard to find. In much of the west, many people are looking for a sense of fulfilment. If the gospel is presented as something that meets this need, well and good; for in a sense, as Augustine discovered, our souls are restless until they find their rest in God. But if this theme is constantly reiterated without any mention of servanthood and death to self-interest, we become guilty of nurturing the very narcissism and hedonism that have corrupted so much of western culture and that stand as glaring indications of our rebellion against God. Again, because society in India is still so highly stratified, believers from the lower levels tend to relate to others in terms of petition and begging, while Christians who are promoted to senior ranks tend to exercise authority in peremptory ways. If the latter group stresses all the texts about heeding the authorities and obeying those who watch for the souls of others, their cultural blind spot will not be healed. They must also listen to injunctions about not lording it over others, about serving as an example, about being the least of all.

Ready examples are easy to find in *every* culture; and Christians in every culture must thoughtfully discover just where their lives have been too greatly shaped by the pervasive influence of their surroundings, rather than by Jesus Christ and his truth. The authentic Jesus consistently overturns many common expectations. Any other Jesus is a sham.

Conclusion

When Jesus really does confront the world, he does so on his own terms; and those terms are not negotiable. People, cultures, movements, values – all are subject to immense change. But the authentic Jesus, however flexible, cannot be pocketed or brought to heel. He makes demands that are personal and costly; he puts spiritual realities before other considerations; he overturns many common expectations; but, thank God, he is always far more wonderful than even his most intimate followers suspect.

> My song is love unknown,
> My Saviour's love to me;
> Love to the loveless shown,
> That they might lovely be.
> O, who am I,
> That for my sake
> My Lord should take
> Frail flesh, and die?
>
> He came from his blest throne
> Salvation to bestow;
> But men made strange, and none
> The longed-for Christ would know.

But O! my Friend,
My Friend indeed,
Who at my need
His life did spend.

Sometimes they strew his way,
And his sweet praises sing;
Resounding all the day
Hosannas to their King.
Then Crucify!
Is all their breath,
And for his death
They thirst and cry.

They rise and needs will have
My dear Lord made away;
A murderer they save,
The Prince of life they slay.
Yet cheerful he
To suffering goes
That he his foes
From thence might free.

In life, no house, no home
My Lord on earth might have;
In death, no friendly tomb,
But what a stranger gave.
What may I say?
Heaven was his home;
But mine the tomb
Wherein he lay.

Here might I stay and sing,
No story so divine;
Never was love, dear King!
Never was grief like thine.

This is my Friend,
In whose sweet praise
I all my days
Could gladly spend.

Samuel Crossman (1624–1683)

The Mission of Jesus

Jesus stepped into a boat, crossed over and came to his own town. Some men brought to him a paralytic, lying on a mat. When Jesus saw their faith, he said to the paralytic, 'Take heart, son; your sins are forgiven.'

At this, some of the teachers of the law said to themselves, 'This fellow is blaspheming!'

Knowing their thoughts, Jesus said, 'Why do you entertain evil thoughts in your hearts? Which is easier: to say, "Your sins are forgiven," or to say, "Get up and walk"? But so that you may know that the Son of Man has authority on earth to forgive sins . . .' Then he said to the paralytic, 'Get up, take your mat and go home.' And the man got up and went home. When the crowd saw this, they were filled with awe; and they praised God, who had given such authority to men.

As Jesus went on from there, he saw a man named Matthew sitting at the tax collector's booth. 'Follow me,' he told him, and Matthew got up and followed him.

While Jesus was having dinner at Matthew's house, many tax collectors and 'sinners' came and ate with him and his disciples. 'When the Pharisees saw this, they asked his disciples, "Why does your teacher eat with tax collectors and 'sinners'?"'

On hearing this, Jesus said, 'It is not the healthy who need a doctor, but the sick. But go and learn what this means: "I desire mercy, not sacrifice." For I have not come to call the righteous, but sinners.'

Then John's disciples came and asked him, 'How is it that we and the Pharisees fast, but your disciples do not fast?'

Jesus answered, 'How can the guests of the bridegroom mourn while he is with them? The time will come when the bridegroom will be taken from them; then they will fast.

'No one sews a patch of unshrunk cloth on an old garment, for the patch will pull away from the garment, making the tear worse. Neither do men pour new wine into old wineskins. If they do, the skins will burst, the wine will run out and the wineskins will be ruined. No, they pour new wine into new wineskins, and both are preserved.'

Introduction

It has been well said that if you aim at nothing you are likely to hit it. That is why parents, for instance, encourage their children to set goals for themselves. People without goals, people without various kinds of purpose, tend to drift from experience to experience, even from crisis to crisis. Their aimless life is easily dissipated in fruitless or even harmful directions, since they have no goals that establish priorities and thereby preserve them from some follies. The best companies and organizations quickly discover the same truth. Any corporation or institution can survive for a little while on the unarticulated dream of the founder or on the surge of the econ-omy; but before long it will fade into irrelevance, if not bankruptcy, unless it repeatedly formulates and reviews its goals.

But goals provide more than aim and incentive. They also provide a set of criteria by which to measure performance. Organized people know this. They carry slips of paper in their pockets with lists of what they intend to do today, or this week, or this month; and as they work through the list, they cross off the completed tasks one by one. This simple action generates enormous satisfaction; but it also provides a kind of check that ensures energy is being *and has been* used wisely. A senior evangelical scholar, known for his prolific pen, carries a list of his current writing projects with him – whether books, articles, or book reviews – and marks them off as he completes them. A father of ten in one of the northern states in America disciplined his children to prepare such lists daily, in order to encourage them to use their time in a disciplined manner. This practice also helps to eliminate false expectations: a few weeks of preparing lists that are extravagantly long and never completed by the day's end soon fosters more realistic goals. Similarly, companies that check what they are doing from time to time against stated goals soon learn to eliminate distracting and time-consuming profit-absorbing sidelines.

In some measure these relations between goals and performance hold true even in the spiritual arena. Of course, one can go too far. I am always a little nervous when I hear of a church setting a goal of, say, 30 percent growth over the next period of time. Doubtless such goals can be set forth in a genuinely spiritual fashion, but too often they are formulated so starkly that it appears the leaders do not believe that conversion is at the end of the day a work of God. It is almost as if the Holy Spirit could get up and walk out and not be missed: the fine machinery would continue to clank on and meet the stated goals.

But before we laugh too hard at these activists, we need to remember that we are morally responsible beings. We have choices to make and priorities to set. For instance, often much praying is not done, whether corporately or by the individual Christian, simply because there has been no real *intention* of praying, no real *plan* to pray. One does not simply drift into a disciplined prayer life. Much evangelism has not been done because we have not aimed to do it. We have not intended to share our faith with our neighbours, or set a goal of getting to know the family across the back fence during the next six months, with the express purpose of loving them for Christ's sake and presenting Christ to them. Something similar could be said about Bible reading. Moreover, to have goals in these areas helps to provide us with criteria by which we can in some measure assess the discipline of our spiritual progress.

Goals, then, are powerful things. It is precisely because of these relationships between goals and performance that when someone wants to take over or redirect a movement or even an individual career, one of the first things he or she does is to meddle with the goals of that movement or career. You see this sometimes in a political party that has lost its way and fallen into considerable disfavor. Then along comes a bright spark who senses the public's mood and decides to capitalize on it. One of the first things he or she may try to do is to restate the party's goals in order to bend the organization to the new mood. Often the organization is willing to go along: the bright spark gains by being supported by the established political machine, and the party gains by being rejuvenated and brought in line with popular concerns.

The same kind of manipulation of goals was attempted in the first century. According to John 6:14–15, some of Jesus' hearers intended to appoint Jesus king by force. They perceived in someone with his miraculous powers the ideal person to take on the Roman overlords and reestablish the kingdom to its long-lost splendor. If they could *force* his hand by appointing him king, even without his formal approval, their agenda would necessarily become his. Once king, he would attract the anger of the ruling overlords; and then he would have to use all of his miraculous powers to extricate himself and the people from the opposition that would ensue.

Satan himself, according to Matthew 4 and Luke 4, attempted to co-opt Jesus by offering him the kingdoms of the world without the pain of the cross. When Peter in Matthew 16 insists that Jesus will never go the way of suffering and death, Jesus recognizes the same source, and responds, 'Get behind me, Satan! You are a stumbling block to me; you do not have in mind the things of God, but the things of men' (Matt. 16:23). The attempt was to foist on Jesus a modified set of goals, a revised mission that eliminated suffering and the cross. But Jesus saw the attempted take-over for what it was, and rejected it with some heat.

There are attempted take-overs of Christianity today as well. If someone wants to bless a movement with the powerful influence of the church, then the first thing to be attempted is a redefinition of the church's mission that turns out, wonder of wonders, to be lined up with the aims of the movement. Marxists have been known to appeal to Acts 2 to show that what Christianity is really about is communal sharing. Marxism is therefore the rightful heir to Christianity. Of course one does not then mention that the sharing of Acts 2 was achieved by the power of transformed lives, and that power was generated by the atonement of Christ and the Spirit he subsequently bequeathed; Marxist sharing depends on what comes out of the end of a machine gun. Right-wing economic and political agendas also try to shanghai the gospel. Did not Jesus say that the truth would set men free, and that he came to give them the abundant life? Jesus is obviously for freedom; the principle extends to the marketplace. That may or may not be good economics; it is a horrible abuse of Scripture. More recently, liberation theology appeals to the exodus as the archetypal freeing of slaves, and Jesus' concern for the poor, to tell us what the Bible is really about. But one wonders why the exodus is chosen. Why not Jeremiah's insistence that the remnant should not rebel against the Babylonian empire? And for all that Jesus displays immense compassion on the poor and the downtrodden, it is remarkable that poverty is never for him the decisive division between those who are accepted and those who are not. When he clears out the temple, for instance, it is not the religious authorities who are chased out but the sellers *and buyers*. The latter certainly included many of the poor – all those who were there to buy the doves, as opposed to the more expensive sacrificial animals.

There have been countless attempts to co-opt the gospel to a cause that, however meritorious, was not itself the proclamation of the gospel. So it becomes extremely important for us to listen to Scripture and to try to articulate the gospel as accurately as possible, to articulate the mission of Jesus. If we succeed in listening to the Scripture on these points, we shall be preserved from the vagaries of every passing theology; more, we shall better grasp the very heart of the faith we profess.

In this series I have been examining what happens and what we may learn when Jesus confronts the world.

In this chapter I want to suggest that the passage before us helps answer the questions: What was Jesus' mission? Why did he come? If the answers it provides are not exhaustive, at least they are crucial.

Why Did Jesus Come?

1. Jesus came to forgive sin and transform sinners; this was foundational to the rest of his ministry (9:1–8).[3] When the people of Gadara pleaded with Jesus to leave their region, preferring pigs to people and wanting swine more than healing (8:34), Jesus acquiesced: he stepped back into the boat he had so recently used, crossed over Galilee, and 'came to his own town' (Matt. 9:1). This, of course, was Capernaum (4:13), right on the lake in an area of fairly high-density Jewish population; so he was immediately plunged back into the vortex of ministry. Matthew does not describe the crowd at this point, nor mention that the only way the friends of the paralytic could reach Jesus was through the roof of the house where he was speaking; typically, he focuses on what is essential to his own narrative. Accordingly he picks up themes that are interwoven throughout these chapters. For instance, the emphasis on Jesus' authority returns (9:6,8; cf. 7:29; 8:9,15,27,29). Similarly, the emphasis on faith – the faith of the centurion (8:10) and the lack of faith among the disciples (8:26) – appears in new guise in the faith Jesus perceives in the friends who carry the paralytic to him (9:2). Jesus 'saw' their faith: that is, he saw their actions in bringing the victim to him, and their actions testified to their faith. Because of *their* faith, Jesus confers great blessings on *the paralytic* – just as today the prayers of faith a believer offers on behalf of another person may benefit the other person.

But the startling new turn in this story that sets it apart from other healing miracles and ties it thematically to the sections that follow begins in verse 2 where Jesus first addresses the paralytic. To the surprise of the onlookers, and probably of the paralytic and his friends, Jesus says, 'Take heart, son; your sins are forgiven.'

The words were unexpected. Here was a paralytic who, on the face of it, came to Jesus to be healed of his paralysis; and Jesus' response seems at best tangential to the man's obvious needs. But closer reflection shows that there are more connections than first meet the eye. Jesus perceives at least two ailments that needed his touch: the paralysis and the sin. Of the two, he clearly judges the latter to be the more important or the more urgent in some way. In the first chapter of this book, we saw that sickness is the consequence of sin – sometimes directly, more commonly indirectly. That is why Jesus' healing ministry pointed to the cross, which deals with sin supremely (8:16–17). But that Jesus should tell this paralytic to take heart from his words strongly suggests that this man's paralysis was the direct result of a specific sin – and the man knew it and laboured under terrible pangs of guilt. Jesus' gentle 'Take heart, son,' as a preface to his 'Your sins are forgiven,' would have been unbearably cruel if the man was aware of no guilt and wanted only to be free of paralysis. But if profound guilt compounded the unutterable weakness, then Jesus' opening words offered the brightest hope. They showed Jesus really understood the man's condition, and was dealing with the deepest hurt. And if the paralysis and some specific sin were so connected, then Jesus' words dealing with sin brought hope that the physical ailment would also be remedied.

But the religious authorities mutter to themselves and entertain dark thoughts about blasphemy (Matt. 9:3).

The verb rendered 'is blaspheming' (viz. Βλασφημεω [*blasphēmeō*]) normally means 'to slander'; but when the one who is slandered is God, the meaning is very close to the modern 'to blaspheme,' and hence the translation here. Some leaders in Jesus' day thought blasphemy occurred only when God's name was invoked and used in an inappropriate way; clearly that is not the case here. In this context, however, the principle is being expanded a little to include demeaning God by claiming to do what God *alone* can do. If I claim to be able to do what only God can do, then I am belittling him by comparing myself with him, and thereby dragging him down to my level.

If this principle applies anywhere, it applies to the question of who may forgive sin. After all, in the last analysis sin is always primarily an affront against God. Others may be hurt, but he is the one whom the rebellious action has most deeply offended. David understood the point: 'Against you, you only, have I sinned and done what is evil in your sight, so that you are proved right when you speak and justified when you judge' (Ps. 51:4). God himself declares, 'I, even I, am he who blots out your transgressions, for my own sake, and remembers your sins no more' (Isa. 43:25; cf. 44:22). Yet here is Jesus, boldly saying 'your sins are forgiven,' though in the eyes of his critics he is certainly not a priest giving absolution and even more certainly not God himself. Whether Jesus knew their thoughts (Matt. 9:4) by some supernatural perception of his own, or simply from the rather obvious shuffling and muttering, makes little difference. Either way he detects the malignant intent of their whispered criticism: 'Why do you entertain evil thoughts in your hearts?' he asks (9:4). It is not so much that their concern to preserve the holiness of God was wrong, as that their inability to grasp Jesus' true identity was in part a moral failure. Then Jesus asks them the question that they should have asked themselves: 'Which is easier: to say, "Your sins are forgiven," or to say, "Get up and walk"?'

The alternatives can easily be misunderstood. What is easier or more difficult is not determined by modern skepticism but by the peculiar brand of skepticism represented by the teachers of the law whom Jesus is confronting. To a modern skeptic, it is doubtless easier to say, 'Your sins are forgiven' than to say, 'Get up and walk'; for the results of the former cannot be tested, whereas the results of the latter will be plain to all. To a contemporary skeptic, talk is cheap. Anyone can absolve another from sin: it is all meaningless. But to command a paralytic to walk again offers the prospect of empirical results to authenticate the potency of the utterance. The teachers of the law in Jesus' day, however, saw the matter in quite another way. They would have immediately insisted that it is far easier to say 'Get up and walk,' than to say, 'Your sins are forgiven.' After all, their own Scriptures offered numerous examples of the kind of person who could say the former. Miracles were credited to Moses, Aaron, Elijah, Elisha, and many, many others. Some of them had even raised the dead. But not one of them had ever granted absolution from sin in so authoritative and unmediated a fashion. That was the more difficult thing by far; for to forgive sin is God's prerogative, and his alone.

In other words, by the rhetorical question Jesus asks, he is claiming to do the more difficult thing, the thing that is God's prerogative. He argues, in effect, that his antagonists should have seen this, and been a little more cautious about accusing him of resorting so easily to blasphemy. But if his utterance was *not* blasphemy, then it is a claim of startling clarity.

If however they are unable to make these connections themselves, he offers them a more direct one. 'But so that you may know that the Son of Man has authority on earth to forgive sins . . .,' he begins, then turns to the paralytic: 'Get up, take your mat and go home' (Matt. 9:6). Matthew tersely comments, 'And the man got up and went home' (9:7). Jesus thus uses the less difficult thing to attest the authority of the more difficult thing. Doubtless the healing was not only a wonderful relief to the paralytic, but also a confirming sign that his sins had indeed been forgiven. To the religious opposition, however, the same miracle is cast as something of a rebuke. They could not credit Jesus' claim to do the harder thing by their direct perception; perhaps they will be able to absorb the point by this less significant display more suited to their capacity. The presupposition is like that found in John 9:30–31: if Jesus had in fact blasphemed when he assured the paralytic that his sins were forgiven, then how could God possibly be granting him the authority to perform this lesser but still spectacular deed? Conversely, if Jesus has the authority to restore a paralytic to full health, even after having assumed the prerogatives of God to forgive sin, then who is to say that the authority he is claiming in the more difficult arena is not also rightfully his?

Even Jesus' use of the 'Son of Man' title is designed to prompt reflection. Like the use in Matthew 8:20, it is purposely obscure: it could simply be a self-reference. But for anyone who remembers that one 'like a son of man' receives a kingdom from God, the Ancient of Days, in Daniel 7, there is at least the potential of linking that promised kingdom with the authority to forgive sin. Certainly Christians made the connection after the cross and resurrection; at this point, the use of the title was pregnant with meaning and vaguely

troubling, but still too opaque for Jesus' hearers to comprehend.

The crowds responded intuitively. They were filled
with fear (not simply 'awe,' as in the NIV). They were
right to be afraid: we *ought* to fear the one who has the
authority to forgive sins. They praised God in terms better than they understood: they praised God, Matthew
records, 'who had given such authority to men' (9:8).
They see in Jesus a man; and they are right. They see in
him a man who exercises God's authority to forgive sins;
and again they are right. Exempt from the theological
hang-ups of the more sophisticated teachers of the law,
they intuitively draw some correct conclusions. But
Matthew's readers know more than the crowds he is
describing. Unlike the crowds, the readers know that
this particular man was virgin-born, engendered of the
Holy Spirit, and called Emmanuel, 'God with us,' in fulfilment of prophecy (Matt. 1). They know that his purpose in coming was to 'save his people from their sins'
(1:21). Jesus is all the crowds said – and much more. God
had indeed given this authority to men – not by simply
delegating it to a particular mortal, but by sending his
Son, virgin-born, to become Emmanuel.

So Jesus did not come simply to heal, or to reign, or to
raise people from the dead. He came to forgive sin, and to
transform sinners. The earlier connection (8:17) between
healing and the atonement confirms that this sin-forgiv-
ing, sinner-transforming ministry was central to everything else that he did. The same point is spelled out in the
next two segments of Matthew 9; and it is decisively
confirmed by the obvious fact that the movement in all
four Gospels is toward the cross and the empty tomb.

Before we press on to the next sections to learn how
this thought is developed, however, it is worth pausing
to reflect how *radical* Jesus' approach really is. During

the 'radical sixties,' when western universities were aflame with many groups of 'radicals' (most of whom have now become yuppies!) telling the world how to sort out all its problems, the president of one Canadian university dropped in from time to time on one or another of the discussion groups sponsored by these 'radical' organizations. At one such meeting, the president, a devout Christian, listened carefully to the presentation and discussion; and to his surprise, at the end of the hour he was asked if he wanted to respond in any way. He replied affirmatively; then he rose, and said that he had hoped to hear some genuinely radical solutions, but was profoundly disappointed to hear nothing but tired old clichés.

That was a profoundly Christian evaluation. Truly *radical* solutions must go to the *radix*, the root of the problem. The sad fact is that as important as it is to attempt political and economic reforms, for example, they are at best temporary, frequently superficial, sometimes merely cosmetic. The Marxist revolution in China has doubtless succeeded in eliminating many of the immense disparities between the haves and the have-nots; but in the process, a new and totalitarian oligarchy has been formed that has been responsible for between twenty and fifty million deaths. No political or economic order can wipe out corruption: what is required is a moral transformation so that society at large judges corruption to be a hideous evil. Then there will only be isolated cases of the problem. Simplistic solutions are not radical; they are reductionistic. Those who advocate a return to nineteenth-century market freedom forget the robber barons, the thousands of immigrants who died building railroads across America, the starvation wages and abysmal conditions in British mines. Marxist theorists, on the other hand, trying to explain the human condition in purely economic terms, keep predicting that once revolutionary man has done his destructive work, the 'new' man of Marxist theory will emerge. He hasn't shown up yet, and he never will; for the theory is wrong. What is at the heart of the human tragedy is not economic injustice but sin. Economic injustice is merely a symptom; and both capitalists and Marxists focus on symptoms and never get near the *radix* at all.

But Jesus does. He is the purest radical. He came to forgive sin, and transform sinners. Where he does his work in abundance, there society is largely transformed.[4] If the next generation, or the one after that, forgets him and knows little of his grace, Christ's people will be reminded of their dependence on him, and recognize afresh that the ultimate solution draws near only when Jesus returns and deals with sin and sinners decisively and finally. Until then the most radical transformations in society take place where Jesus does his pardoning and transforming work. Jesus came to forgive sin and transform sinners; and this was foundational to the rest of his ministry. That is why Christians, who have begun to appreciate the immense liberty in experiencing God's pardon, sing lustily:

> Great God of wonders! all thy ways
> Are worthy of thyself, divine;
> And the bright glories of thy grace
> Among thine other wonders shine:
> > Who is a pardoning God like thee?
> > Or who has grace so rich and free?
>
> Pardon from an offended God!
> Pardon for sins of deepest dye!
> Pardon bestowed through Jesus' blood!
> Pardon that brings the rebel nigh!

Who is a pardoning God like thee?
Or who has grace so rich and free?
O may this glorious, matchless love,
This God-like miracle of grace,
Teach mortal tongues, like those above,
To raise this song of lofty praise:
Who is a pardoning God like thee?
Or who has grace so rich and free?

Samuel Davies (1723–1761)

*2. Jesus' central ministry, the forgiveness of sin, meant that he
came to call the despised and disgusting elements of society
(9:9–13).* The first event in this section is the call of
Matthew. The 'tax collector's booth' at which he sat was
probably a customs and excise booth at the border
between the territories of Herod Antipas and Philip, not
far from Capernaum. Tax collectors were not held in
high esteem. The tax farming system meant corruption
was widespread; and to many politically conservative
Jews, tax collectors were almost traitors since they were
serving the ends of the overlords, not the Jewish people
themselves. Moreover the higher echelons of Jewish tax
collectors would necessarily have dealings with their
Gentile superiors, and this would almost certainly put
them in situations where they would be contaminated
by ceremonial uncleanness. But Jesus called Matthew to
follow him; and Matthew obeyed. It has been pointed
out, rightly, that Matthew's post meant he had to be flu-
ent in Aramaic and Greek, and accustomed to keeping
accurate records – characteristics that later stood him in
good stead when, so far as we can tell from the external
evidence, he kept notes on Jesus' ministry and eventually penned this Gospel.

The focus of interest in this verse, however, is not on
Matthew's scribal habits, but on the resulting dinner at

which many tax collectors and 'sinners' joined Matthew and Jesus. The quotation marks around the word *sinners* in the New International Version is a way of drawing attention to the fact that these people were sometimes so designated by the Pharisees and others, even when they were simply common folk who did not share all the Pharisees' ceremonial scruples. But the term also included other, more disreputable people – harlots, shysters, renegades on the outskirts of Jewish life. They are all lumped together in the mind of the Pharisees, who are deeply offended that Jesus and his disciples should actually be eating with them. Jesus and his followers could scarcely do so without risking ceremonial defilement; but just as bad, they were keeping company with the wrong sort of people. Can you not tell a person's character by the company he keeps? Isn't it true that if you live with garbage you will smell like garbage? Besides, when the Messiah comes, won't he side with the righteous and the good, build them up and promote them, and purify the land and nation of its disgusting elements?

Jesus' response brings us to the heart of the dispute between him and some of his chief opponents. 'It is not the healthy who need a doctor, but the sick' (9:12), he says; and then he adds to his case by citing Scripture. The expression he uses to introduce the quotation, 'go and learn,' was a rabbinic formula used in a slightly sardonic way to administer a gentle rebuke to those who needed to go and study the text of Scripture further. Jesus' opponents, who prided themselves in their knowledge of Scripture and their own conformity to it, needed to 'go and learn' what it meant.

The quotation itself is from Hosea 6:6: 'I desire mercy, not sacrifice.' In the context of Hosea's day, God was telling the religious leaders and nobles through his prophet that although they continued the temple ritual at full tilt they had lost the center and heart of their God-given religion. From God's perspective, they were apostate, despite their observance of religious formalities. They had forgotten that the God whom they claimed to serve was the compassionate God who had delivered them from Egypt, graciously given them the covenant at Sinai, disclosed himself to them in countless ways, provided a sacrificial system by which their sin might be atoned for, cared for them and disciplined them as they learned the lessons of obedience and gradually took possession of the Promised Land, and promised them a deliverer, a Messiah, who would bring to pass all of his rich promises to them. God in mercy had sought them, called them, and constituted them a nation. Now, Jesus says, he too has come with the same heart: 'I have not come to call the righteous, but sinners' (9:13).

What this means, of course, is that Jesus by quoting this passage is not simply saying that the Pharisees ought to be more compassionate, but that he aligns them with the apostates of ancient Israel. Like those whom the prophet Hosea condemned, Jesus' opponents have in his view preserved the shell and lost the core. Their attitude to tax collectors and 'sinners' simply proves the case. This also means that when Jesus says 'I have not come to call the righteous, but sinners,' he is *not* suggesting that the Pharisees are genuinely righteous and without need of him. He is not dividing the world's population into righteous and unrighteous, and insisting he came only for the latter. After all, he has just lumped these 'righteous' Pharisees with Israel's apostates! That Jesus does not think the righteousness of the Pharisees to be adequate is made clear elsewhere in this book, when Jesus insists that to enter the kingdom one must possess righteousness that exceeds that of the Pharisees and teachers of the law (Matt. 5:20).

The point of verse 13*b* is not to divide humanity into two groups, the righteous and the unrighteous, but to disavow one image of what the Messiah would be and do, and replace it with another. The saying gives us the essential nature of Jesus' messianic mission as he himself saw it. His mission was characterized by grace, by a pursuit of the lost. Contrary to the expectations of some of his opponents, he did not come to establish the righteous and destroy the sinners (as they established these categories), but (still using their categories) to win sinners. By implication, those who do not understand Jesus' mission as he himself does, and who therefore exclude themselves from the list of 'sinners' because they see themselves as 'righteous,' can have no part in the messianic bounty Jesus is beginning to introduce.

In short, Jesus' central ministry, the forgiveness of sin, meant that he had to entangle himself with sinners. He came to call the despised and disgusting elements of society. When today those who promote themselves as righteous view religion through the prism of their self-justification, Jesus says in effect that he did not come for them. Their understanding of what the Christian religion is all about is so warped that the only way he can even begin to make them understand is to insist that he came for the very people whom they despise and find repugnant. Against the broader canvas of Jesus' teaching, however, including the powerful rebuke that links these self-righteous people with ancient apostates, what this means is that, if they but realized it, these 'righteous' people are really nothing of the kind.

It turns out that the people who think they are *worthy* of Messiah's *attention* are no more worthy than the socially repulsive people whom they dismiss. And both kinds of people are in *need* of his *mercy*, even if they are not *worthy* of his *attention*. From this perspective, when we say that Jesus came to call the despised and disgusting elements in society, it turns out that no one is exempt. Christ came, as Calvin puts it, 'to quicken the dead, to justify the guilty and condemned, to wash those who were polluted and full of wickedness, to rescue the lost from hell, to clothe with his glory those who were covered with shame, to renew to a blessed immortality those who were debased by disgusting vices.' But then, is any of us exempt? And if we think we are, we face not only the conclusion that Christ did not come for us, but also the intense rebuke that aligns us with the apostates of old.

There are at least three practical lessons to be drawn from this passage.

First, Christians must learn profound gratitude for the salvation that has won them. Contrary to popular opinion, genuine Christians do not think of themselves as better than other people. Indeed, many converts discover, within a few short weeks of their conversion, that their hearts are more deceptive and sinful than they ever thought possible. That is a common aftermath of conversion: the euphoria (if there was any) gradually dissipates, to be replaced by a puzzling and growing sense of sin. The reason is obvious to more mature Christians: growing conformity to Jesus Christ, the powerful work of the Spirit within us, soon shows up the level of our self-centeredness. Attitudes and reactions we display that never troubled us in the past now appear as abominations. But there is an immense benefit. Our growing awareness of the magnitude of our sin can only result in growing thankfulness for the richness of the pardon we have received. When we are reminded that Jesus said, 'I have not come to call the righteous, but sinners,' far from being offended, we are relieved.

Second, Christians will also learn from Jesus' example. We will not develop a posture of supercilious self-righteousness toward those whom society dismisses; for we know that Jesus came to call the despised and disgusting elements of society. Not only so, we know that includes us; and as we get to know our own hearts better, we begin to realize that there is scarcely a sin we cannot conceive of committing ourselves, if only our circumstances, parents, upbringing, and the like had been different, if only we had not tasted the elixir of forgiveness from our pardoning God.

There is a story of a Christian woman who visited a condemned Nazi officer after Nuremburg. That officer had been responsible for the brutal deaths of her parents and siblings, and for her own torture. She had heard that he was deeply repentant; and when she approached him he wept and begged her for forgiveness. Her initial reaction was bristling rage: How dare he ask for forgiveness when his crimes were so heinous? Would his pathetic tears bring back her family? Was forgiveness so cheap?

And then she remembered that forgiveness is never cheap. If the grace of God could not extend to this Nazi officer, then it was insufficient for her; and she needed it as much as he. Because she had been forgiven, she also frankly forgave.

Christians can never afford to adopt haughty stances toward other sinners. They are never more than poor beggars telling others where there is bread.

Third, there is immense hope in this passage for the person who would like to follow Christ, but who does not feel good enough. The simple truth is that if you feel good enough for Jesus he does not want you. He came for the sick and the sinful, the broken and the needy. He invites sinners to him; and he forgives them and transforms them. He does so because he died and rose again *for sinners*. That is why the church sings:

> Come, ye sinners, poor and needy,
> Weak and wounded, sick and sore;
> Jesus ready stands to save you,
> Full of pity, love, and power:
> He is able,
> He is willing; doubt no more.
>
> Now, ye needy, come and welcome;
> God's free bounty glorify:
> True belief and true repentance,
> Every grace that brings you nigh,
> Without money,
> Come to Jesus Christ and buy.
>
> Let not conscience make you linger,
> Nor of fitness fondly dream;
> All the fitness he requireth
> Is to feel your need of him:
> This he gives you –
> 'Tis the Spirit's rising beam.
> Come, ye weary, heavy-laden,
> Lost and ruined by the Fall;
> If you wait until you're better,
> You will never come at all;
> Not the righteous –
> Sinners Jesus came to call.
>
> View him prostrate in the garden,
> On the ground your Maker lies!

On the awful tree behold him,
Hear him cry before he dies.
It is finished!
Sinner, will not this suffice?
Lo, the incarnate God, ascended,
Pleads the merit of his blood;
Venture on him, venture wholly,
Let no other trust intrude:
None but Jesus
Can do helpless sinners good.

Joseph Hart (1712–1768)

And while the church sings this, the person who under the crush of guilt hungers for forgiveness and relief, hears that Jesus came for sinners and sings:

No, not despairingly
Come I to thee;
No, not distrustingly
Bend I the knee:
Sin hath gone over me,
Yet is this still my plea,
Jesus hath died.

Ah, mine iniquity
Crimson hath been,
Infinite, infinite,
Sin upon sin:
Sin of not loving thee,
Sin of not trusting thee,
Infinite sin.

Lord I confess to thee
Sadly my sin;

All I am tell I thee,
All I have been:
Purge thou my sin away,
Wash thou my soul this day;
Lord, make me clean.
Faithful and just art thou,
Forgiving all;
Loving and kind art thou
When poor ones call:
Lord, let the cleansing blood,
Blood of the Lamb of God,
Pass o'er my soul.

Then all is peace and light
This soul within;
Thus shall I walk with thee,
The loved Unseen;
Leaning on thee, my God,
Guided along the road,
Nothing between.

Horatius Bonar (1808–1889)

3. As part of his effective dealing with sinners, Jesus came to set up a new structure that could embrace the profound reality he was introducing (9:14–17). Doubtless John the Baptist himself was free from petty jealousy when he saw how superficially popular Jesus and his ministry became. Unfortunately, there is ample evidence that not all of John's disciples were so large-hearted. Sometimes they complained to him (John 3:26–36); sometimes, as here, they approached Jesus himself and found fault with his ministry, making common cause with the Pharisees in the process. In one sense, it was easy for them to do so on this point; for their master, the Baptist himself, had clearly been an ascetic, so on matters of fasts the Baptist's disciples and the Pharisees enjoyed a more or less common perspective.

Jesus' answer is profoundly christological – that is, its validity depends entirely on who he himself is. 'How can the guests of the bridegroom mourn while he is with them? The time will come when the bridegroom will be taken from them; then they will fast' (Matt. 9:15).

What kind of person can say, in effect, 'Be happy; for I am here!'? I know of a little girl who, when she was about two and a half, went to visit a home for senior citizens that she and her mother had visited before. Remembering how happy many of these senior folk had been to see her the last time, she burst into the common room, flung wide her arms, and cried, 'I'm here!' The extraordinary self-centeredness of a child is forgiven, even indulged, precisely because, ironically, it is so ingenuous. But an adult could not take the same approach, except perhaps on a slapstick comedy show. Yet here is Jesus adopting just such a stance.

In fact, the implicit christological claim is even stronger than it first appears, because of the metaphor of the bridegroom to which he appeals. According to the fourth Gospel, John the Baptist had applied the same metaphor to Jesus: John himself was the best man (to use modern terminology), while Jesus was the bridegroom (John 3:29). But the roots of the metaphor go back to the Old Testament. Commonly it is applied to God himself, in his relationship with his covenant people: 'For your Maker is your husband – the LORD Almighty is his name – the Holy One of Israel is your Redeemer; he is called the God of all the earth' (Isa. 54:5; cf. 62:4–5; Hos. 2:16–20). Jews in Jesus' day sometimes applied the metaphor to the long-awaited Messiah; and the messianic banquet that marked the full coming of the messianic age was this bridegroom's

wedding feast. That notion is picked up in the New
Testament (e.g., Matt. 22:2; 25:1; 2 Cor. 11:2; Eph.
5:23–32; Rev. 19:7,9; 21:2). The language Jesus uses is
cryptic enough that probably not even his closest disciples fully understood what he was talking about until
after the resurrection; yet in fact he was claiming to be
the Messiah, and that his presence marked the dawning of the messianic age. That, he says, is reason
enough why his disciples should not fast.

There was another enigma built into his saying. Jesus
says that the time will come when he will be taken away;
and then it will be appropriate for his disciples to fast.
Of course, this side of the cross and the resurrection, we
understand what he meant, and we remember the tears
that were shed by the early band of disciples until they
found the tomb was empty and then touched and saw
and ate with their Master. But at the time Jesus said these
words, when no one around him, not even his most intimate followers, understood that though he was king of
Israel yet his mission would take him to the cross, Jesus'
saying recorded in this verse must have been almost
incomprehensible. Just when even the opponents might
suspect that Jesus was making a messianic claim, he
spoke of being taken away, and causing his disciples
grief. But would the genuine Messiah be taken away?
Would the disciples of the genuine Messiah begin their
experience with him in joy, and end it in sorrow? Like so
many of Jesus' utterances, this one too was necessarily
cast in somewhat veiled terms that would be fully
explained only after the cross and resurrection had
become history.

But if Jesus is the Messiah, what difference would it
make so far as fasting and other Jewish religious practices are concerned? Verse 15 shows it ought to make a
personal difference: that is, his very presence is cause for

joy and a suspension of some religious practices of a mournful nature. But verses 16–17 show that in addition to these personal differences there will also be large *structural* differences introduced to the practice of religion. The lesson is spelled out in two parables, each a slice of life. The first takes place in the sewing room: 'No one sews a patch of unshrunk cloth on an old garment, for the patch will pull away from the garment, making the tear worse' (Matt. 9:16). To repair a large rent in an old and well-shrunk cloth, it is necessary to use a patch that is similarly well-shrunk. The two parts must be compatible. The second parable takes place in a wine cellar: 'Neither do men pour new wine into old wineskins. If they do, the skins will burst, the wine will run out and the wineskins will be ruined. No, they pour new wine into new wineskins, and both are preserved' (9:17). Skin bottles for carrying various fluids were normally made by killing and skinning an animal, sewing up all orifices, fur side out, after tanning the skin with special care to reduce the possibility of disagreeable taste in the liquid to be stored. Eventually such a skin bottle became brittle. If new wine, still fermenting, were stored there, the fermentation gases could easily exert enough pressure to split the bottle. New wine was therefore placed in new wineskins, if at all possible, because they would still be pliable and somewhat elastic, and therefore less likely to split open.

What this means, of course, is that the new wine Jesus is introducing simply cannot be stored in the old wineskins of the structures of Judaism. The old structures could not stand the pressure. New structures would have to be used in conjunction with this new wine.

The dimensions of this claim are nothing less than astonishing. Here is someone who is proposing to overturn the prevailing structures of Jewish religion, on the

ground that they are inadequate to contain the new revelation and the new situation he himself is introducing. The
contents of the new revelation are not here spelled out; but
they are not hard to deduce, partly from the rest of this
Gospel, and partly from the way other New Testament
writers have fleshed out the skeleton. Matthew's Gospel
has already been at pains to show that Jesus and the kingdom he is introducing are the *fulfilment* of Old Testament
expectations, promises, and structures. Elsewhere we are
told that if Jeremiah promises a new covenant (Jer.
31:31ff.), we are driven to the conclusion that even some
Old Testament writers recognized the principial obsolescence of the Mosiac covenant (Heb. 8:13). If the Psalms
promise a new priest who does not spring from the tribe
of Levi, but who is a messianic figure serving in the order
of Melchizedek (Ps. 110:4), then necessarily there is envisaged an overthrow of the Mosaic legislation as it then
stood; for the Levitical priesthood is so interwoven with
that legislation, its tabernacle (later temple) rites, its sacrificial system and feasts, that a new priesthood unavoid-
ably means a new covenant (Heb. 7). Paul insists that in
any case the gospel he preaches is in direct line with and
fulfilment of the covenant with Abraham, a covenant that
was not overturned when the Mosaic law was introduced
centuries later. The Mosaic covenant was in certain
respects a training period until the promised Redeemer
arrived (Rom. 4; Gal. 3). Acts 2 insists that Pentecost is the
fulfilment of Joel's prophecies about the universal distri-
bution of the Spirit; and this expectation, both in Joel and
elsewhere (e.g., Ezek. 36), marks the end of the tribal, representative nature of the old covenant, and the beginning
of a new age and arrangement between God and his people. Jesus himself elsewhere insists that the time was at
hand when the focal point for worship would no longer
be Jerusalem (John 4); and if not Jerusalem, then not the

temple; and if not the temple, then not the sacrificial system. Without the sacrificial system, the Mosaic covenant is necessarily transmuted into something unrecognizable. Indeed, Jesus insists that he is the temple, the new and real meeting place between God and man (John 2:19–22; cf. Matt. 26:61).

Now of course little of this is spelled out in detail in Matthew; still, the careful reader cannot help but spot adumbrations of this structure even within the teaching of Jesus. When he instituted what we call the Lord's Supper he spoke of the blood of the new covenant. He repeatedly claimed, sometimes with greater and sometimes with lesser clarity (largely dependent on the circumstances in which he found himself), to be the promised Son of man, the predicted Messiah, the fulfilment of prophetic hopes and expectations. And though he himself was born under the written law and took pains to obey it, he not infrequently spoke in ways that anticipated its obsolescence.

In short, the verses before us (Matt. 9:14–17) insist that Jesus came to bring revelation and introduce a situation so new that the very structures of antecedent revealed religion would change. It will not do to suggest, as some have done, that because Jesus says, at the end of this parable, that 'both are preserved' that he envisages the legitimate preservation of *both* Judaism *and* the new religious structures he is introducing. For in the categories of the parable, the 'both' that are preserved are not the *old* wineskins and the new wine, but the new wineskins containing the *new* wine. In other words, Jesus envisages the preservation of the new revelation that he himself was introducing, and the new structures, the new forms of religious expression, the new covenantal relationships, that would embrace it.

Jesus is not simply another Abraham or Moses, another Elijah or Jeremiah. All of biblical revelation comes to its focus in him. Nor is this a conclusion of the later church, foisted back on him – a theological conclusion of which he was blissfully unaware. Far from it: in the Gospels he operates out of a profound self-awareness that understood his own authority to be nothing less than divine, that understood his own mission to be the culmination of centuries of revelatory preparation. This is the authentic Jesus; unless we see him in this light, and obey him and worship him as he is presented to us in Scripture, we shall be guilty of manufacturing a false Jesus, a Jesus with different goals and purposes from the ones the authentic Jesus actually held and exemplified.

Conclusion

What was Jesus' mission? Why did he come? He came to save his people from their sin; he came to transform sinners. He did not come to call the righteous, but sinners. And this mission required the establishment of new forms of religious expression, changes to the existing covenantal structure between God and his people, to accommodate the new reality being introduced. No longer would priests offer daily, weekly, monthly, and yearly sacrifices that covered sin over; now one sacrifice would deal finally and effectively with sin. No longer would the meeting place between God and man be localized in a temple in Jerusalem; now it would be 'localized' in the person of God's Son. No longer would the Spirit be poured out only on the leaders of the covenant community; now all the heirs of the new covenant would know the Spirit's work for themselves. And if the final fruition of Jesus' mission must await his return, then at least we may rejoice that the principal dealing with sin has already taken place in Jesus' initial mission – even if the consummation of his work awaits his return.

Suppose you heard of a medical doctor who discovered an infallible cure for cancer. Would you not want to bring to him anyone you knew who was suffering from this dreaded disease? Suppose, further, that he could heal Alzheimer's disease, reverse all cardiopulmonary disease, and eliminate dependence on alcohol. Suppose in addition he were a brilliant economist who, quite demonstrably, advanced solutions that removed tensions between the haves and the have nots, but did so in such an equitable way that all sides were pleased. Suppose, further, that he was so politically astute and forceful that he advanced satisfactory solutions to the most intractable problems: Northern Ireland, Afghanistan, the Middle East. Would you not think the world would beat a path to his door?

But quite apart from the fact that many would not want his solutions if they adversely impinged on their own selfish desires, we must conclude that this mythical person cannot hold a candle to Jesus and all that he provides. For Jesus is eventually going to do all these things anyway. He will one day introduce a new heaven and a new earth, where there will be no more disease, no more war or injustice. But he will do so *because he has already dealt foundationally with the root problem, the problem of sin.* That is why the various attempts to domesticate Jesus by redefining his mission in order to swing the weight of the church behind some contemporary cause are so pathetic. The resulting Jesus is not authentic, merely an idol. The resulting solutions are not stable, but at best temporary and at worst ephemeral. The resulting religion is without power to transform, but is merely formal. And the resulting expectations are invariably dashed.

Not so the real Jesus. He came to forgive sin and transform sinners; he founded the church as the ongoing display of his covenant people and the agent to proclaim his truth and manifest his power; and he comes again to bring his sin-cleansing, life-transforming work to completion. That is God's plan; that is the mission of Jesus.

> Blessed be God, our God!
> Who gave for us his well-beloved Son,
> The gift of gifts, all other gifts in one–
> Blessed be God, our God!

> What will he not bestow,
> Who freely gave this mighty gift un-bought,
> Unmerited, unheeded, and unsought –
> What will he not bestow?

> He spared not his Son!
> 'Tis this that silences each rising fear;
> 'Tis this that bids the hard thought disappear –
> He spared not his Son!

> Who shall condemn us now?
> Since Christ has died, and risen, and gone above,
> For us to plead at the right hand of love,
> Who shall condemn us now?

> 'Tis God that justifies!
> Who shall recall the pardon of the grace,
> Or who the broken chain of guilt replace?
> 'Tis God that justifies!

The victory is ours!
For us in might came forth the Mighty One;
For us he fought the fight, the triumph won –
The victory is ours!

Horatius Bonar (1808–1889)

4 (Matthew 9:18–34)

The Trustworthiness
of Jesus

While he was saying this, a ruler came and knelt before him and said, 'My daughter has just died. But come and put your hand on her, and she will live.' Jesus got up and went with him, and so did his disciples.

Just then a woman who had been subject to bleeding for twelve years came up behind him and touched the edge of his cloak. She said to herself, 'If I only touch his cloak, I will be healed.'

Jesus turned and saw her. 'Take heart, daughter,' he said, 'your faith has healed you.' And the woman was healed from that moment.

When Jesus entered the ruler's house and saw the flute players and the noisy crowd, he said, 'Go away. The girl is not dead but asleep.' But they laughed at him. After the crowd had been put outside, he went in and took the girl by the hand, and she got up. News of this spread through all that region.

As Jesus went on from there, two blind men followed him, calling out, 'Have mercy on us, Son of David!'

When he had gone indoors, the blind men came to him, and he asked them, 'Do you believe that I am able to do this?'

'Yes, Lord,' they replied.

Then he touched their eyes and said, 'According to your faith will it be done to you'; and their sight was restored. Jesus warned them sternly, 'See that no one knows about this.' But they went out and spread the news about him all over that region.

While they were going out, a man who was demon-possessed and could not talk was brought to Jesus. And when the demon was driven out, the man who had been mute spoke. The crowd was amazed and said, 'Nothing like this has ever been seen in Israel.'

But the Pharisees said, 'It is by the prince of demons that he drives out demons.'

Introduction

Like many parents with young children, we read quite a lot to our two. What we read varies from the sublime to the ridiculous, or at least to the humorous. Standing rather closer to the latter side than to the former is a little book called *Alexander and the Terrible, Horrible, No Good, Very Bad Day*.[5] I cannot hope to convey the marvelous pictures to you; but let me cite a few paragraphs:

> I went to sleep with gum in my mouth and now there's gum in my hair and when I got out of bed this morning I tripped on the skateboard and by mistake I dropped my sweater in the sink while the water was running and I could tell it was going to be a terrible, horrible, no good, very bad day.

At breakfast Anthony found a Corvette Sting Ray car kit in his breakfast cereal box and Nick found a Junior Undercover Agent code ring in his breakfast cereal box but in my breakfast cereal box all I found was breakfast cereal.

I think I'll move to Australia.

In the car pool Mrs Gibson let Becky have a seat by the window. Audrey and Elliott got seats by the window too. I said I was being scrunched. I said I was being smushed. I said, if I don't get a seat by the window I am going to be carsick. No one even answered.

I could tell it was going to be a terrible, horrible, no good, very bad day.

At school Mrs Dickens liked Paul's picture of the sail-boat better than my picture of the invisible castle.

At singing time she said I sang too loud. At counting time she said I left out sixteen. Who needs sixteen?

I could tell it was going to be a terrible, horrible, no good, very bad day.

I could tell because Paul said I wasn't his best friend anymore. He said that Philip Parker was his best friend and that Albert Moyo was his next best friend and that I was only his third best friend.

I hope you sit on a tack, I said to Paul. I hope the next time you get a double-decker strawberry ice-cream cone the ice cream part falls off the cone part and lands in Australia.

There is much more along this vein. I shall not spoil the book for you by telling you how it turns out. Certainly Alexander was learning, among the myriads of life's little tragedies, that friends are frequently fickle. School alignments shift and shift again. Especially when people move around are old alliances broken and new ones formed. The other day I was trying to think of one person with whom I was reasonably close when I was an undergraduate at McGill University, who is still a close friend today. I could not think of one. The person with whom I was closest preceded me to seminary. We often prayed together, and worked at evangelism and Bible studies together. But in time our ways parted. He subsequently apostasized, and then later tragically committed suicide.

Often enough in the business arena the same dislocation of friendship occurs. Perhaps a friend is promoted, and suddenly becomes supercilious, condescending, or aloof. Even marriage, a God-ordained institution that ought to generate the most marvelous intimacy, sometimes turns friends into acquaintances, acquaintances into enemies. Friends are not always trustworthy.

Indeed, this question of trustworthiness is not tied exclusively to friendship. How often do we idolize someone, raise him to the proportions of majestic statuary, only to discover the statue has clay feet. We marvel at our idol's integrity and candour, and then discover he cheats on his income tax. We praise his courtesy and charm, and find out he is abusive to his wife. We admire her beauty, mature restraint, and competence, only to learn she is making a cuckold of her husband.

Even in the best of circumstances, we are likely to be disappointed. Long-time and cherished friends and spouses can still cause hurt. Indeed, part of maturity as a human being is learning how to accept human frailty.

And then suddenly, with chagrin, we recognize that human frailty begins with us; we remember with shame the many people whom we have disappointed or otherwise hurt. And we wonder if genuine trustworthiness can be predicated of anyone.

But Christians rightly sing:

> One there is above all others,
> Well deserves the name of Friend;
> His is love beyond a brother's,
> Costly, free, and knows no end:
> They who once his kindness prove,
> Find it everlasting love.
>
> *John Newton (1725–1807)*

In our study of Matthew 8 – 10, we have been considering what happens when Jesus confronts the world. I want to suggest to you now that one of the things that stands out whenever this confrontation occurs is the sheer trustworthiness of Jesus.

This is not what happens in many other confrontations. Too often both sides sacrifice their integrity on the altar of victory. Political manipulation becomes more important than honesty; it is not only in war that truth is the first victim. In academic confrontation, a thesis may be followed by antithesis, which is then followed by personal abuse. Teenagers in a family start a squabble, and pretty soon each side is looking around for weapons that will really hurt. He yells, 'Pimple face!' and she yells back, 'Fatty!'

But there is in Jesus a center, an integrity, a fidelity that makes him utterly trustworthy. I shall sketch in:

Four Facets of Jesus' Profound Trustworthiness

1. Jesus is trustworthy with respect to the purposes for which he came. After all, one cannot be trustworthy in the abstract. One must be trustworthy with respect to an assignment, a mission, a responsibility, an obligation. Jesus is trustworthy, then, with respect to the purposes for which he came, the mission that we surveyed in the last chapter.

The point is made by several features in Matthew's presentation of Jesus' miracles. The sequence of miracles in chapters 8 – 9 is, of course, topically arranged, as is clear by comparing the parallel reports in the other synoptic Gospels. Together, as we have seen, they underline several important themes, including the authority of Jesus and the mission of Jesus. But the last three miracles reported in these chapters, the ones we shall now look at more closely, bear their own special importance. The first is a miracle of resurrection from the dead (9:18–19, 23–26), to which the healing of the woman with the hemorrhage is attached (9:20–22); the second is the healing of the blind men (9:27–31); and the third is the exorcism and consequent healing of the mute (9:32–34). But these three kinds of miracles – raising the dead, healing the blind, and making the dumb speak – are specifically taken up just a couple of chapters later. There, John the Baptist, languishing in prison and troubled that Jesus is not taking strong action to bring about justice in the land, sends envoys to Jesus to ask him if he is the one who was to come, or if they should expect someone else (11:2). Jesus replies with words evocative of Isaiah 35:5–6 and 61:1, but referring specifically to the miracles he has already performed: 'Go back and report to John what you hear and see: The blind receive sight, the lame walk, those who have leprosy are cured, the deaf hear, the dead are raised, and the good news is preached to the poor. Blessed is the man who does not fall away on account of me' (Matt. 11:4–6).

Clearly, then, the miracles of Matthew 8 – 9, and not least these last three, have prepared the way for Jesus' response. In a sense, therefore, they supply us with some of Jesus' messianic credentials. He performs them, and they are recorded, to demonstrate that Jesus is indeed the one predicted by Old Testament prophets. Jesus must prove trustworthy in meeting the strictures of that role.

This same rather simple but no less important point is made by the way Matthew condenses the account of the healing of the ruler's daughter (Matt. 9:18–19, 23–26). If we compare the parallel account in Mark 5:21–24,35–43, we discover far more details. The ruler was a synagogue ruler by the name of Jairus. There were crowds of people all around; and when Jairus first approached Jesus, his daughter had not yet died. A little farther on, after the healing of the woman with the hemorrhage, some men came from Jairus's house with the news the girl was dead. We are provided with an exact list of which persons were permitted to accompany Jesus to the dead girl's side and witness the miracle. Jesus' exact words in Aramaic are preserved. But little of this is found in Matthew, who eliminates the details of little interest to the principal point he wishes to make. Even with respect to the little girl's death, Matthew condenses, as one author puts it, 'so as to present at the outset what was actually true before Jesus reached the house' – a standard of reportage common enough in the Gospels. But Matthew preserves the details about the mourners, since they serve as witnesses that the girl is in fact dead. In that culture, even a poor family was expected to provide a couple of flute players and at least one professional wailing woman to set the right tone for the loud lamentations that testified to the passing of the dearly beloved. The synagogue ruler's daughter, clearly, was dead – in fact, so clearly was she dead that the crowd laughed at Jesus when he seemed to suggest otherwise (9:24).

With this clean, stripped-down account of the miracle, then, there is not much left except the miracle itself – which of course is one way of focusing attention on that miracle. Jesus as the Messiah is doing what some Old Testament prophets said the Messiah would do.

The same emphasis is almost certainly bound up with the 'Son of David' title used by the blind men when they called out to Jesus for help: 'Have mercy on us, Son of David!' (9:27). That title is used by Matthew in the very first verse of this Gospel: Matthew begins with a record of the genealogy of 'Jesus Christ *the son of David*, the son of Abraham' (1:1; emphasis added) – clearly a messianic title. But many of the occurrences of the title throughout the book are bound up with healings and exorcisms. In addition to the one here in Matthew 9, we find a substantial list. The Canaanite woman cries to Jesus, 'Lord, Son of David, have mercy on me! My daughter is suffering terribly from demon-possession' (15:22). In 20:30, we read of two more blind men crying, 'Lord, Son of David, have mercy on us!' Other occurrences are no less clearly messianic. In Matthew 21, the children cry in exuberant praise, 'Hosanna to the Son of David!' (21:9,15); and in 22:41–46, in a discussion with the Pharisees over the meaning of Psalm 110, Jesus clearly presupposes that the Messiah is both the Son of David and David's Lord.

In all of these instances, then, the people who were addressing Jesus in this way were petitioning him as *the Messiah*. The blind men in the chapter before us, for instance, may not have had a very nuanced theological understanding of the Old Testament; but their need drove them to confessions that might not have been attempted if they were both whole and sophisticated. Perhaps they reasoned like this: We have heard of the wonderful healings this man from Nazareth has performed. Perhaps he is indeed the Messiah. Do not the Scriptures look forward to a time when the eyes of the blind will be opened and the ears of the deaf unstopped

(Isa. 35:5)? What have we got to lose by asking him for help? If he ignores us, we shall not be worse off than we already are. If he hears us and heals us – ah, then we shall have our heart's desire!

And so their desperation drove them, as the exuberance of the children in Matthew 21 drove them, to appeal to Jesus as the Son of David. Though blind, they 'saw' better than some who could see only with their eyes. Need and desperation, like poverty of spirit (Matt. 5:3), are often the first steps in the pathway of faith.

That is the sort of reasoning that the blind men probably adopted; but Matthew himself is less interested in their psychology than in the christological confession itself. His point is simple: these blind men rightly addressed Jesus as the Son of David, the Son of David introduced in the very first verse of this book; and Jesus then performed the miracle that confirmed the attestation. Just as the healing of the paralytic confirmed that Jesus has authority to forgive sins (9:1–8), so here the healing of the two blind men confirms that Jesus is the promised Son of David, the Messiah, who brings with him the blessings of the kingdom. Jesus is faithful to discharge all the functions that are bound up with his mission. Failure to do so would mean he was untrustworthy in the mission for which he was sent. And that is Matthew's elementary and repeated point.

That simple truth – that Jesus truly is the promised Messiah, and is utterly trustworthy in discharging all that is bound up with that mission – should be a marvelous encouragement to believers today. If he came to save his people from their sin (1:21), will he not do so? If his purpose as the Messiah is to bring in the blessings of the consummated kingdom, will he not achieve it? If even now his mission is to give foretastes of what it will be like when both sin and the effects of sin are removed by his life-transforming authority, shall we not witness such foretastes ourselves? He is utterly trustworthy in meeting the purposes for which he came; and those purposes are bound up with the good of his people.

2. Jesus is trustworthy even in the face of scorn and slander. On the face of it, this is a rather easy and obvious point; but it is one with some important ramifications for us.

The scorn is found in the laughter of the crowds when Jesus tells them, 'Go away. The girl is not dead but asleep' (9:24). Doubtless they thought the great healer had come too late. Intoxicated by his success, he would try out his skills on a corpse, and make a fool of himself. In fact, Jesus' words are very important; and even if they were not well understood at the time, they became much clearer after his own resurrection. 'Sleep' is not infrequently a euphemism for death (Dan. 12:2; John 11:11; Acts 7:60; 1 Cor. 15:6,18; 1 Thess. 4:13–15; see also 2 Peter 3:4); but since sleep is here *contrasted* with death, something more must be meant. If 'sleep' in this context is precisely the equivalent of death, then Jesus' statement reduces to something like, 'Go away. The girl is not dead but dead.' Nor will it do to suppose that Jesus was referring merely to the physical reality: everyone else had thought she was dead, but they were wrong, for in reality she was, quite literally, only asleep. If that were all that was meant, this miracle would hardly have been special, and Jesus would have been ill placed to list, among his credentials, that 'the dead are raised' (11:5).

The least that Jesus meant by this contrast between sleep and death was that in this instance the real death of the girl was not as final as the mourners thought. In his presence, before his authority, death itself must flee. Death is reduced to not much more than sleep. Implicitly there may also have been a criticism of the

Sadducean view that said there was no resurrection (cf. 22:23). In any case, Jesus' statement can be understood only if we see that he is less interested in making a medical diagnosis than in making a christological claim. When Jesus confronts our last, great enemy, death itself, death is the loser. It is stripped of its power and reduced to sleep.

Like many of Jesus' utterances, this one was guarded, even mysterious, in its initial context. The mourners exhibited neither the spiritual discernment nor the emotional sympathy that might have pierced through to Jesus' meaning. What it earned him at the time was scorn. Yet this does not deter him from his course. Another might have withdrawn in a huff, offended by the coarse rejection, and unwilling to serve in a context of such skepticism; but not Jesus. Indeed, part of his mission *was to be rejected!* Even his perseverance under attack becomes a microcosm of the suffering of the cross that lay ahead.

Something similar must be deduced from the slanderous attacks recorded at the end of this section of Scripture. After Jesus had driven the demon out of the mute, the 'crowd was amazed and said, "Nothing like this has ever been seen in Israel"' (9:33). Unfortunately, there was another opinion: 'the Pharisees said, "It is by the prince of demons that he drives out demons"' (9:34). In short, their official view was that if Jesus could control demons, he was in cahoots with them.

From the point of view of the Pharisees, this was a comforting explanation. The claims of Jesus could then be dismissed; even the evidence of the wonderful works he performed could be ruled out. Satan himself might be prepared to suffer a few tactical losses for a greater strategic end. Doubtless that was why the same criticism was levelled against Jesus again and again. In chapter

12, for instance, when some are asking if Jesus could indeed be the Son of David (12:23), the Pharisees argue: 'It is only by Beelzebub [one of the names given to Satan], the prince of demons, that this fellow drives out demons' (12:24). Jesus' answer, in part, is that Satan can hardly afford to continue in this vein; for he would in fact be destroying his kingdom, his household. And in any case, Jesus puts the alternative explanation of his miraculous power in straightforward terms: 'if I drive out demons by the Spirit of God, then the kingdom of God has come upon you' (12:28). His point is that if the Pharisees' dismissive charge does not stand up, there is really only one alternative; and that alternative entails the conclusion that the promised kingdom of God has dawned. It has arrived and is operating among the people. It 'has come upon you.'

Thus Jesus' opponents sometimes directly misrepresented his motives and maligned his miracles. He came from the Father; they said he came from the devil. His authority was God's; they said it was demonic. He came in fulfilment of Scripture; they believed he was perverting Scripture. For most of us, it is very hard to persevere with calm integrity when we are so thoroughly misunderstood, so systematically slandered. However, Jesus not only proved trustworthy in the face of scorn and slander, but also did so precisely because it was part of his mission to do so. The movement is toward the cross.

What we must recognize, however, is that this pattern of behaviour is not to be dismissed as relevant only in the case of Jesus, but is something we too are called to emulate. It is to this very slander – that Jesus was the agent of the prince of demons – that he refers in 10:24–25: 'A student is not above his teacher, nor a servant above his master. It is enough for the student to be like his teacher, and the servant like his master. If the head of the house has been called Beelzebub, how much more the members of his household!'

The point, of course, is that as followers of Jesus we cannot expect to be treated better than he was. It would be unreasonable to think otherwise. If the world judges us narrow, bigoted, or mad, that is only to be expected. At least the world does not usually accuse us of being in cahoots with the devil! Part of our growing trustworthiness as Christians will be reflected in our ability to handle opposition, scorn, and slander in the same way that Jesus did.

3. Jesus is trustworthy, whether the faith of others to apprehend him be great or small - provided only that it issues from need and is focused on him. Doubtless this point needs explaining; but once understood it becomes an immensely stabilizing factor in a Christian's faith.

We may begin by observing that faith has already played a fairly important role in these three chapters. The centurion (8:5-13) displayed *great* faith. He understood, as we saw in the first chapter, that Jesus stood between God and man in much the same way that a centurion stood between Rome and the common foot soldier. Because of the chain of authority in both cases, when the centurion spoke, Rome spoke; and when Jesus spoke, God spoke. The analogy may not have been perfect; but the centurion had penetrated deeply into the nature of Jesus' authority, so much so that Jesus himself was surprised by the greatness of the man's faith.

On the other hand, in 8:25-26 we saw an example of poor faith, bankrupt faith. Here the disciples cry in desperation as the ferocious storm threatens to capsize their boat; and they are so un-discerning that they can actually entertain the supposition that Jesus the Messiah might die in a squall. Surely if their faith had penetrated, even a little, to who he really was, they would have recognized how impossible it was for the Lord from heaven to have his mission destroyed by a freak boating accident! Their faith was very poor. Yet even so, Jesus performed the miracle that calmed their fears.

When we turn to the passage before us, we find two more references to faith; and in both instances faith is portrayed in a somewhat novel guise. In the first (9:20–22), we encounter the woman with the hemorrhage. Once again Matthew strips the story down to its essentials. The seriousness of the woman's condition is briefly noted: she has suffered for twelve long years. If the bleeding was from her womb, then according to Jewish law she would have been considered unclean for that entire period. Strictly speaking, she should not have been in this crowd, where she could be contaminating many others; and most certainly she should not have been touching Jesus. Her faith is mingled with superstition: she thinks touching a piece of cloth can heal her. She is like the people in Acts 5 who think that they will receive some special blessing or miraculous help if only Peter's shadow could pass over them.

Mingled with superstition or not, her faith is honored, and she is healed. Indeed, Jesus draws attention to her faith: 'Take heart, daughter,' he says, 'your faith has healed you.'

Finally, in the healing of the two blind men (9:27–31), Jesus asks the men if they really *believe* he is able to meet their request (9:28): presumably this is a device to increase and focus their faith. When they reply in the affirmative, Jesus says, 'According to your faith will it be done to you' (9:29); and their vision is restored. This cannot mean that the miracle would be executed *in proportion* to their faith – as if Jesus were saying, 'So much faith, so much sight; 50 percent faith, 50 percent sight.

Believe wholly and 20/20 vision will be restored to you.'
The 'according to' language does not deal with propor-
tionality here, but with factuality: in line with your faith,
which believes I can restore your sight, let your sight be
restored.

The diversity of these exhibitions of faith drives us to
an important conclusion. In one sense, it is not faith that
heals, that saves, that transforms. It is Jesus who does
that. He is the one who has the authority; he is the one
who is inaugurating the kingdom. The faith is effective
only as a *means* is effective. In that sense, Jesus rightly
says to the hemorrhaging woman that her faith has
healed her. But he does not mean that it is faith in and of
itself, irrespective of faith's object. The faith that saves is
the faith whose object is Jesus; and in reality it is Jesus
who saves.

Now it is clear why the different degrees and kinds of
faith mentioned in these chapters prove effective.
Whether it is the great faith of the centurion, or the bankrupt faith of the disciples, or the superstitious faith of the
hemorrhaging woman, or the hopeful messianic faith of
the two blind men – in each case the faith *is directed
toward Jesus, and is an expression of need*. Such faith is necessary to apprehend the blessings Jesus brings; at the
end of the day, it is not so much the strength or purity of
the faith that is at stake, but whether or not faith issues
from self-acknowledged need, and is directed to the one
who has the power to meet that need, the Lord Jesus
Christ himself.

After all, there is little virtue in faith in the abstract. If
my faith has as its object Krishna, or the sacred mush-
room, or Marxist hope for a better world completely free
of struggle and injustice, then by all biblical evidence my
faith is worthless. It may have some power to drive my
life in a unified direction and give it some kind of

subjective meaning; but because its object, in the light of biblical revelation, is unworthy of such faith, the faith itself is not commendable. Faith must be founded on fact: the truthfulness of the revelation of Jesus Christ is everywhere presupposed. Elsewhere, when the Corinthians seem to be calling in question the resurrection of Jesus Christ, Paul goes so far as to say that if they are right then our Christian faith is futile (1 Cor. 15:17). He will not acknowledge as valid that faith whose object is not real, true, and in conformity with the revelation that Jesus Christ is and brings. On the other hand, as James 2:19 points out, if faith has a proper object but is merely credal, then the devils themselves can be said to believe – but with no benefit to them. Faith not only must have a proper object, but also must issue from need and be characterized by genuine trust and obedience.

Faith in some merely abstract sense, then, is not presented in Scripture as an unqualified virtue, any more than sincerity is. Doubtless sincerity is better than insincerity; but one may be simultaneously sincere and entirely mistaken. There is no reason to doubt the sincerity or the faith of the prophets of Baal who opposed Elijah, crying out and cutting themselves to win their god's attention.

The real virtue, then, is not in faith itself so much as in that which faith rightly apprehends. That is why the varieties of faith displayed in the chapters before us all produce fruit: at least they have this in common, that they issue from need and turn to Jesus for help. And Jesus, the object of faith, provides the help. That in turn means the crucial element is not the strength of our own faith, but *the trustworthiness of Jesus*. To reiterate the main point: Jesus is trustworthy, whether the faith of others to apprehend him be great or small – provided only that it issues from need and is focused on him.

An example from the Old Testament will clarify the point. It is the night of the first Passover. Mr Smith and Mr Jones, two Israelites who have observed the succession of plagues that have befallen Egypt and sometimes spilled over into the land of Goshen where most of the Israelites lived, are having a conversation over the back fence.

Mr Jones confesses his deep worries over the coming night: 'Of course I'm concerned. Shouldn't I be? God has sent waves of plagues: flies, frogs, darkness, water turning to blood. But this latest announcement is frankly terrifying. The loss of the firstborn in every household in Egypt! The nation will be shattered.'

'But haven't you done what Moses said, and daubed the side posts and lintel with blood from the paschal lamb?'

'Of course. I'm an Israelite, just like you. But a bloodstain or two seems a strangely weak way to stop the ravages of the angel of death. I'm terrified for my son, and I don't know what else I can do to ensure his safety.'

Mr Smith sighs. 'You've done all you need to, all you can do. You know that I've got a son, too, and I'm perfectly confident that he is safe. God has promised through Moses that in households where the blood has been applied as stipulated, the first-born male will be safe. Don't you think God will keep his word? Where is your faith?'

When Mr Jones replies, he is hesitant and troubled. 'Please don't give me moralizing sermons about faith. I'm scared, and that's all there is to it. I've sprinkled blood around, just as God said; but I'm frightened for my son, and I wish I could do something to guarantee his safety.'

That night the angel of death passed through the land. In most houses there was loud weeping and wailing, as the first-born males died in huge numbers throughout the land. Now the question is this: Which man, Mr Smith or Mr Jones, lost his first-born son?

The answer, of course, is: Neither. Mr Smith had great faith; Mr Jones displayed rather anemic faith. But both had shown enough faith to daub the blood on the door posts and lintel. Beyond that, the outcome depended utterly on the reliability of the promises of God.

Something very similar is portrayed in the Gospels, and especially in these three chapters. We do not wrench blessings from Jesus by somehow increasing the intensity of our faith. Granted we have any genuine faith at all, what is far more important is the faithfulness of Jesus. And ironically, when we focus on that, we find our own faith strengthened as we come more greatly to appreciate the one on whom our faith rests.

4. *Jesus is trustworthy, even when some seek to sidetrack his mission.* There were always enough people around who, wittingly or unwittingly, were trying to sidetrack that mission.

In the first chapter, in thinking about Matthew 8:4, we noticed that Jesus enjoined silence on the man he cured of his leprosy. With miracles as spectacular as his, it was not always possible to keep things quiet. News of the raising of Jairus's daughter, we are told, 'spread through all that region' (9:26). Perhaps it was because of his spreading fame as a miracle-worker that Jesus refrained from dealing with the two blind men until they were all indoors (9:28), away from the fervent enthusiasm of the crowd. Reports of privately performed miracles would of course leak out; but such reports were less likely to excite uncontrolled enthusiasm than those done in full view of a large and expectant audience – in much the same way that reports of a favorite rock group will prove less exciting to a vast crowd of teenagers than a performance by the gyrating pop stars themselves. Concern that he *not* be perceived as simply another miracle-worker, concern that his messiahship *not* be reduced to many of the popular expectations of the day, was doubtless the primary reason Jesus enjoins silence on the two healed men who had been blind (9:30). Their discourtesy and disobedience in spreading the news about him 'all over that region' (8:31) cannot obliterate the fact that Jesus himself took concrete steps to forestall misrepresentation of his ministry, which could have warped it and steered it off in another direction, sidetracked from the mission on which the Father had sent him.

This is not a case of reading too much out of too little; for the danger of being sidetracked is one Jesus recognizes at the outset of his public ministry, one that he has to confront again and again. The heart of the temptations dangled before him by the devil himself (Matt. 4:1–11) was the prospect of kingly rule *without continued submission to the Father's plan, including the path to the cross.* That is why Jesus responded so firmly when Peter had the audacity to suggest that the cross should have no part in Jesus' agenda (16:21–23). Gethsemane itself was nothing but the agonizing desire to escape the cup he was committed to drink (26:39). Even on the cross itself, in the midst of the most awful shame and rejection, Jesus was buffeted with the temptation to escape the pain and ignominy, and prove his credentials, by the jeers of bystanders who 'hurled insults at him, shaking their heads and saying, "You who are going to destroy the temple and build it in three days, save yourself! Come down from the cross, if you are the Son of God!"' (27:39–40).

But if popularity and the attendant acclaim of the masses could not seduce Jesus or veer him from his course, neither could shame, mockery, and the self-conscious attempts to sidetrack him from his mission. As his ministry progresses and the opposition mounts, Jesus becomes more and more set on the course he is pursuing.

How unlike much of our own drift! There are few religious leaders who are not spoiled by acclaim, and even fewer who keep their perspectives and integrity when under intense fire. But Jesus proves utterly trustworthy, even when some seek to sidetrack his mission.

Conclusion

Now all of these observations lead to one final point of great importance. The pattern of Jesus' trustworthiness is displayed in one way or another in all the Gospels, and sometimes referred to in other New Testament books (e.g., Heb. 3:1ff.). Behind this pattern stands one cardinal truth: *Jesus Christ is trustworthy first and foremost because he is faithful to his Father.*

Implicitly, of course, we have recognized this truth when we have said that Jesus is always faithful to his mission; for his mission is not simply *his* mission, as if it were something he rather willfully decided to take up on his own, but *the Father's* mission entrusted to him. He came, above all, to do the Father's will. Even the dark hour in Gethsemane does not find Jesus crying, 'Help me to love these sinners more! Help me to prove trustworthy to them!' – but rather, 'My Father, if it is possible, may this cup be taken from me. Yet not as I will, *but as you will*' (Matt. 26:39; emphasis added).

The same pattern is found elsewhere. In John's Gospel, for example, Jesus says, 'The one who sent me is with me; he has not left me alone, for I always do what pleases him' (John 8:29). Even more stunning is John 14:31: 'the world must learn that I love the Father and that I do exactly what my Father has commanded me.'

This does not mean that Jesus and his Father are engaged in some sort of private transaction in which the interests of humanity are of little concern. The point is that the mission of the Son is to save sinners. God so *loves* the world that he sends his Son; the Son comes to give his life a ransom for many. But it does mean that we ought not weigh the trustworthiness of Jesus purely in terms of what he does for us, nor purely in terms of his personal relationship with his Father, but in the profound truth that the interpersonal relationships of the Godhead, so far as we know them, are directed toward the redemption of men and women from every tongue, tribe, people, and nation. It is in the context of his redemptive purposes that we experience Jesus' great love for us. To continue the words of the poem by John Newton that introduced this chapter:

> Which of all our friends to save us,
> Would consent to shed his blood?
> But our Jesus died to have us
> Reconciled in him to God:
> This was boundless love indeed!
> Jesus is a Friend in need.
>
> When he lived on earth abased,
> Friend of sinners was his name;
> Now, above all glory raised,
> He rejoices in the same:
> Still he calls them brethren, friends,
> And to all their wants attends.

Could we bear from one another
What he daily bears from us?
Yet this glorious Friend and Brother
Loves us, though we treat him thus:
Though for good we render ill,
He accounts us brethren still.

O for grace our hearts to soften!
Teach us, Lord, at length to love;
We, alas, forget too often
What a Friend we have above!
But when home our souls are brought,
We shall love thee as we ought.

Nevertheless, that trustworthiness and redemptive love of Jesus that we enjoy is displayed as a function of Jesus' fidelity to his Father's redemptive plan. If we know that his love for poor sinners is utterly trustworthy, it is because Jesus' love for his Father is perfectly trustworthy.

O, the deep, deep love of Jesus!
Vast, unmeasured, boundless, free;
Rolling as a mighty ocean
In its fullness over me.
Underneath me, all around me,
Is the current of thy love;
Leading onward, leading homeward,
To my glorious rest above.

O, the deep, deep love of Jesus!
Spread his praise from shore to shore;
How he loveth, ever loveth,
Changeth never, nevermore;
How he watches o'er his loved ones,
Died to call them all his own;

How for them he intercedeth,
Watcheth o'er them from the throne.
O, the deep, deep love of Jesus!
Love of every love the best:
'Tis an ocean vast of blessing,
'Tis a haven sweet of rest.
O, the deep, deep love of Jesus!
'Tis a heaven of heavens to me;
And it lifts me up to glory,
For it lifts me up to thee.

S. Trevor Francis (1834–1925)

And that brings us to the subject of the next chapter.

5 (Matthew 9:35 – 10:15)

The Compassion
of Jesus

Jesus went through all the towns and villages, teaching in their synagogues, preaching the good news of the kingdom and healing every disease and sickness. When he saw the crowds, he had compassion on them, because they were harassed and helpless, like sheep without a shepherd. Then he said to his disciples, 'The harvest is plentiful but the workers are few. Ask the Lord of the harvest, therefore, to send out workers into his harvest field.'

He called his twelve disciples to him and gave them authority to drive out evil spirits and to heal every disease and sickness.

These are the names of the twelve apostles: first, Simon (who is called Peter) and his brother Andrew; James son of Zebedee, and his brother John; Philip and Bartholomew; Thomas and Matthew the tax collector; James son of Alphaeus, and Thaddaeus; Simon the Zealot and Judas Iscariot, who betrayed him.

These twelve Jesus sent out with the following instructions: 'Do not go among the Gentiles or enter any

town of the Samaritans. Go rather to the lost sheep of
Israel. As you go, preach this message: "The kingdom of
heaven is near." Heal the sick, raise the dead, cleanse
those who have leprosy, drive out demons. Freely you
have received, freely give. Do not take along any gold or
silver or copper in your belts; take no bag for the journey,
or extra tunic, or sandals or a staff; for the worker is
worth his keep.

'Whatever town or village you enter, search for some
worthy person there and stay at his house until you
leave. As you enter the home, give it your greeting. If the
home is deserving, let your peace rest on it; if it is not, let
your peace return to you. If anyone will not welcome
you or listen to your words, shake the dust off your feet
when you leave that home or town. I tell you the truth,
it will be more bearable for Sodom and Gomorrah on the
day of judgment than for that town.'

Introduction

Little is more tiring than constant service to people –
even constant exposure to people. When we have not
mixed with people for a while, we long to be with them;
when we have been with too many people for too long,
we need to be by ourselves. That is one reason why families that live in the country, sometimes many miles from
their nearest neighbour, tend to be open and eager to
welcome the passing stranger. The hospitality of country
folk is proverbial. But if you live in the heart of London
or New York, you will see thousands and thousands of
people on the streets every day, and be aware of millions
more; and then your tendency will be to treat your flat
as an enclave that visitors may approach only with care.
If the Englishman's home is his castle, the city-dweller's

home is his private, fortified castle. The person who arrives unannounced and unexpected is not likely to be given a warm reception.

The same problem of too much exposure to people is likely to bedevil the couple where one spouse spends most of the day with hordes of people and the other spends the day largely alone. Come evening, the first wants to stay home or, at the most, spend a quiet evening with intimate friends; the other wants to talk, socialize, invite friends in, go to a party perhaps.

In one sense, the burnout we feel when we hear of yet more suffering, famine, and disaster on the nightly news stems from the same sort of exposure. Before the advent of the mass media, the ordinary family was called upon to worry about local conditions and affairs, and only occasionally about national and international matters – for instance, when one of the men was called up to serve in the military. The news normally received about international events was months or even years late. But today, a few shots can be fired anywhere in the world, and we are called to worry about them that evening on the news. We become tired; our compassion seems to dry up as we are called upon to exercise it again and again, with no seeming change in the nature of the news. We harden ourselves a little, and find it easier to philosophize about evil and suffering than to weep over it or do much about it.

Anyone who has engaged in extensive public ministry knows that emotional burnout is a great danger. When it takes place, genuine ministry is traded for mere professionalism. The high goals with which we began may dissolve in the acid bath of sheer need. We may become more proficient; but we may also become more mechanical, less compassionate.

Jesus faced the same pressure. He 'went through all the towns and villages' of Galilee, we are told (9:35), 'teaching in their synagogues, preaching the good news of the kingdom and healing every disease and sickness.' According to Josephus, a Jewish historian writing about a generation after Jesus, there were 204 cities and villages in Galilee, each with no fewer than fifteen thousand persons. Even if the latter figure is applicable only to the walled cities, and not to the villages (which is not what Josephus says), a conservative estimate points to a very large population, even if smaller than the three million that Josephus's figures indicate. If Jesus were to speak in two towns or villages a day, it would still take about four months to canvass the lot. Quite apart from the sheer energy needed to keep up such a pace was the emotional drain of serving more and more people who pressed to hear him and see him. This pressure was at least part of the reason why on another occasion he felt it necessary to withdraw from the crowds and attempt to escape by boat across the lake – only to be thwarted in this plan by the crowds of people who ran around the north end of the lake, crossed at the fords, and met him as he disembarked. Whatever the success or failure of this attempt to retire for a while, Jesus certainly recognized the need for rest.

Nevertheless, Jesus' basic stance towards the vast numbers of people who pressed in on him was compassion. Immediately after the summary of Jesus' strenuous ministry, Matthew recalls: 'When he saw the crowds, he had compassion on them' (9:36).

I began to understand what this attitude looks like about twenty years ago, when I was trying to begin a church in the west end of Ottawa. The work was slow and discouraging, and there were times I wanted to get away from it. The pastor who was supervising me, a chap called Ken Hall, suggested one evening that we go for a swim at a lake nearly forty miles back in the hills. I eagerly anticipated the evening. The water was always clean, there were seldom many people up there, and a raft was tethered several hundred yards out that made a convenient target for a lazy swim. To my horror, when we arrived we found the beach covered with hundreds of teenagers. They were having a very noisy beach party to celebrate high-school graduation. High-decibel sound equipment belted out the latest rock music so forcefully that residents in Ottawa probably had to shut their windows in self-protection. Not a few of the young people were already drunk, and the combination of celebration, booze, and bathing suits guaranteed that the public necking would be only a shade less than obscene.

Deeply disappointed that my evening's relaxation was being shattered by a raucous party, I was getting ready to cover my disappointment by moral outrage. I turned to Ken to unload the venom, but stopped as I saw him staring at the scene with a faraway look in his eyes. And then he said, rather softly, 'High-school kids – what a mission field.'

In one sense, he had seen and heard exactly what I did; in another sense, we had not seen and heard the same things at all. The difference was not in the objective reality, but in his compassion. I had much to learn.

Of course, rest is necessary. But Christians can never treat the relationship between ministry and rest in the same way that the world treats the relationship between work and holidays. Many see vacations as the *end* or *purpose* of work, and even of life itself. Their work *earns* a holiday; they then *deserve* a vacation. When they return from their two or three weeks, they hate the thought of going back to work; and they can hardly wait for the next set of holidays. By contrast, the Christian loves to serve. Ministry of all kinds is the *end*, the *purpose*; holidays are simply a means to that end. Far from serving in order to earn a rest, we take rests now and then in order to serve the better. That means, of course, that if a planned rest doesn't work out just as we had expected, and more ministry intervenes, we cannot be frustrated or bitterly disappointed. Our times are in the Father's hands; he well knows the rest can be delayed a little if there is need for urgent ministry.

In other words, compassion in ministry is not so much the characteristic of a certain type of personality, as the characteristic of the person with a certain set of *priorities*. If we forget that our task is to minister *to people*, compassion will no longer be the characteristic of our life, but a quality we try to turn on and off depending on whether or not we think we should be 'on duty.'

When Jesus confronts the world, one of the features that stands out most starkly is his compassion. In the verses before us we shall notice several aspects of this compassion.

Reflections on the Compassion of Jesus

1. Compassion is Jesus' fundamental response to varied human needs. When Jesus saw the crowds, we are told, 'he had compassion on them, because they were harassed and helpless, like sheep without a shepherd' (9:36).

It is important to see, first, that Jesus seems to be especially touched by the masses and their needs precisely *because* they are leaderless, harassed, bullied, bruised, helpless. Like sheep without a shepherd, they are exploited, adrift, moving as a flock but rarely knowing why or where. The activity that we might berate as mindless he sees as the result of being leaderless. The mass fads and hysteria that we write off as immature and ignorant he can therefore treat with compassion. The resentments, rebellion, diverting amusements, foolish pastimes, raw hooliganism, and stupid habits can be condescendingly dismissed by the elite of society; but Jesus' diagnosis implicitly puts not a little of the blame on those who are so dismissive. Behind the objectionable behavior, indeed the sinful behavior, lie frustration, exploitation, unarticulated despair at not knowing which way to turn. Where, then, are the leaders? The sad truth is that they are often in the same state as the led – which is another way of saying they are not real leaders at all. In other instances they are too busy worshiping themselves; in still others, far from helping or leading the masses, they contribute to the sheer harassment of the people.

That is what Jesus sees when he contemplates the great crowds; and according to Matthew, that is why he is moved to compassion. It is a commonplace of Scripture that God brings comfort to the downcast and succor to the downtrodden. 'He has brought down rulers from their thrones but has lifted up the humble. He has filled the hungry with good things but has sent the rich away empty' (Luke 1:52–53). This ties in rather tightly with Jesus' summary of his own mission: 'It is not the healthy who need a doctor, but the sick' (Matt. 9:12). It is almost as if Jesus is drawn to those who are most put upon, those who are suffering and exploited, those who are most aware of their needs and who hope that he can meet them. Is it not the poor in spirit who inherit the kingdom of God?

I am preparing these lines in England, to which I have returned after an absence of a couple of years. As I settle down to reading the newspapers and hearing the television news readers, I detect a subtle change in the atmosphere. That change is marked by the decay of hope.

Two years ago, British commentators recognized, of course, many of the problems that confront the country: rising racial tensions, high unemployment, loss of standing in the world community so far as productivity, trade balances, and standard of living go; rising cultural pluralism that threatens to rend the fabric of the nation, continuing strife in Northern Ireland – and, at the time, a coal miners' strike of breathless hate and barely suppressed violence. But even so, sturdy British resilience was not far beneath the surface. Britain has weathered storms in the past: it can handle this one as well.

Now the commentators are not so sure. Pessimism surfaces as Britain falls lower in the ranks of the European Economic Community, as its educational system produces too few scientists and engineers (and too many of the best of their ranks cannot find adequate employment and therefore emigrate). There are so few heroes, notes *The Times*, that there is a moment of national rejoicing when Botham rejoins the cricket team against New Zealand, following his suspension for smoking marijuana. More and more editorials sound bleak. Hope is gradually dying.

But in one sense, this may provide Christians with an opportunity that comes only where there is a sense of loss and ferment. It is rare that Christians earnestly seek the Lord's face when things are going swimmingly, when material blessings abound and we seem to be protected from the vicissitudes faced by others. But in the blackness of discouragement, when we are harassed and downcast, we may indeed turn to the Lord and acknowledge our helplessness apart from his grace; we may do so knowing that God is a compassionate God, and that Jesus' compassion was particularly directed toward the harassed and the helpless.

But second, it is no less important to see that in the context of the Gospel of Matthew Jesus, by exercising his compassion, in no way relinquishes his moral stance. With us, it is so often the case that compassion and moral outrage prove incompatible: the one devours the other. The compassion generates excuses for those to whom the compassion is directed, and the high ground of holiness is somehow lost. Or the expression of concern for holiness, rightly refusing to make excuses for sin, wrongly refuses to be compassionate as well, and falls headlong into self-righteousness.

But with Jesus it is not so. If we place this passage within the context of all of Matthew, we discover with delight that Jesus recognizes the prevalence and vileness of sin, yet is compassionate. The book as a whole pictures Jesus coming to save his people *from their sin* (1:21). In the Sermon on the Mount, Jesus simply assumes that people are evil: for example, 'If you, then, though you are evil, know how to give good gifts to your children, how much more will your Father in heaven give good gifts to those who ask him!' (7:11). Even Jesus' healing ministry, as we saw in the first chapter of this book, was exercised as a function of his principal handling of the problem of sin (8:17); for he did not come to call the righteous, but sinners (9:13). Jesus dares to articulate moral outrage (see especially Matt. 23); but the same Jesus weeps over the city of Jerusalem.

Third, Jesus' compassion is here cast in a metaphor that betrays more than compassion. The people, Jesus laments, are 'like sheep without a shepherd' (9:36). The language calls to mind the rich array of Old Testament passages in which either God or God's promised Messiah is the compassionate shepherd who will come to lead, feed, and protect God's people. At one point, God promises, '"I will place over them one shepherd, my servant David [written hundreds of years after David's death, so the reference must be to great David's greater Son], and he will tend them; he will tend them and be their shepherd. I the LORD will be their God, and my servant David will be prince among them. I the LORD have spoken . . . You my sheep, the sheep of my pasture, are people, and I am your God, declares the Sovereign LORD"' (Ezek. 34:23–24,31; cf. 37:24). Matthew himself cites Micah 5:2: '. . . out of you will come a ruler who will be the shepherd of my people Israel' (Matt. 2:6). Again, in connection with his death, Jesus cites Zechariah 13:7: '"I will strike the shepherd, and the sheep of the flock will be scattered"' (Matt. 26:31). Preserving the same metaphor, Jesus in the passage before us sends the disciples 'to the lost sheep of Israel' (10:6).

Inevitably, then, biblically literate Christian readers, thinking through the report of Jesus' words after the fact, detect not only compassion but another messianic allusion. Jesus' very compassion toward 'sheep without a shepherd' qualifies him as the shepherd they need, the shepherd long promised in Scripture who (as Matthew has carefully noted) would be born in Bethlehem and truly tend the flock of God.

In short, compassion is Jesus' fundamental response to varied human need. This compassion is not diluted by other responses equally fundamental, and complementary to his profound compassion. Rather, it rises the more starkly to the fore, and serves to authenticate his messiahship as faithfully and powerfully as any miracle.

2. The compassion of Jesus issues in a call to pray. 'When he saw the crowds,' we are told, 'he had compassion on them . . . Then he said to his disciples, "The harvest is plentiful but the workers are few. Ask the Lord of the harvest, therefore, to send out workers into his harvest field"' (9:36–38). The metaphor changes from sheep farming to harvest, as Jesus tries to arouse in his disciples compassion similar to his own. The word harvest does not here mean 'harvest time,' as often in the Gospels, and then associated with judgment (e.g., 13:49; cf. Isa. 17:11; Joel 3:13). Rather, it means 'harvest crop,' a point made clear by the word *plentiful*. If the 'harvest' is 'plentiful,' it must be the harvest crop that is in view. Stripping the metaphor away, Jesus is saying that there is a large number of people in some sense simply waiting to hear the gospel of the kingdom. The fields of people are ready, waiting to be harvested. They are urgently in need of workers to go and proclaim the good news to them.

What, then, should be done? Should we begin with training sessions to enable us to multiply the evangelizing force? Should we plot a major strategy of recruitment? Should we found a few strategically placed seminaries? Or perhaps we should begin by establishing two or three international foundations to help pay for these plans?

At some point or other, all of these may be good steps to take. But they are secondary steps, not to be attempted until considerable energy is poured into the first step. And the first step is to pray – to pray to the Lord of the harvest, that *he* would send out workers into *his* harvest field. One commentator puts it this way: 'As no man will himself become a sincere and faithful minister of the gospel, and as none discharges in a proper manner the office of teacher, but those whom the Lord raises up and endows with the gifts of his Spirit, whenever we observe a scarcity of pastors, we must raise our eyes to him to afford the remedy.'

The world is full of wickedness, whether in the first world or the third, the second or the fourth; whether in 'civilized' areas or more primitive situations; whether in the democracies or under totalitarian regimes; whether in countries where there is a great deal of 'churchianity' or in countries where raw animism still dominates. Who is sufficient to meet such needs? Shall lives and whole societies be transformed by mere oratory, or merely by the power of doing good deeds? Nothing will suffice but the power of God; and therefore we must entreat him to work.

Nevertheless, the work we are to entreat him to perform, according to Jesus, is that he raise up workers! Doubtless we could have asked him to save a lot of people; doubtless that is a fine prayer. But it is not the focus here. God *normally* works through *means*; and that is why we are to pray to God, asking him to raise up the workers, the means, to spread the gospel and to display the power of the kingdom. This is *not* the same as mere recruitment and training; for the workers *God* raises up will be endowed by him with the gifts and graces necessary to meet this enormous challenge. The workers we commission who do not enjoy this divine endowment will not be much more than functionaries, and may actually do considerable damage by confusing thousands and thousands of people as to what Christian work is really all about.

The centrality of prayer in the purposes of God surfaces at many crucial places in the Bible. One of them was instrumental in my own sense of call to the ministry. While working in a Canadian government chemistry laboratory, trying to tackle a certain problem in air pollution, I gradually became more concerned with moral pollution than with air pollution, more interested in biblical truth and its application to men and women than in the application of scientific discoveries to our daily lives. I am not for one moment suggesting that Christians cannot serve the Lord in the context of the natural sciences. On the contrary, this is my Father's world, and

Christians need to be involved in every part of it. But for me, the focus of interest and compulsion began to change. Doubtless God was quietly working in my life, through reflection, the counsel of friends, early opportunities for ministry that came my way, and other means. Toward the end of this period of uncertainty, I heard someone preach a sermon on Ezekiel 22. I remember very little of that sermon; I remember the text vividly. There God lists the gross corruptions of ancient Israel, especially of the aristocracy, of the merchants and of the prophets. Toward the end of the catalog we read, 'Her officials within her are like wolves tearing their prey; they shed blood and kill people to make unjust gain. Her prophets whitewash these deeds for them by false visions and lying divinations. They say, "This is what the Sovereign LORD says" – when the LORD has not spoken. The people of the land practice extortion and commit robbery; they oppress the poor and needy and mistreat the alien, denying them justice' (Ezek. 22:27–29).

But the most searing indictment of all comes in the final words of the chapter. God says, in what appears to be a combination of profound sorrow, deep disgust, and holy indignation, 'I looked for a man among them who would build up the wall and stand before me in the gap on behalf of the land so I would not have to destroy it, *but I found none*. So I will pour out my wrath on them and consume them with my fiery anger, bringing down on their own heads all they have done' (22:30–31; emphasis added). Clearly, the man the Lord looked for was not in the first place a candidate to prophetic or priestly ministry; he was someone who would 'stand before *me*' – that is, someone who would stand before the Lord as an intercessor. The account of Moses comes to mind in the episode of the golden calf: he intervened on behalf of the people, begging God not to wipe them out, beseeching God to have mercy on them. But when God looked at his people this time, he could not find anyone who would exercise that role. Not one.

I wish I could say that I have always been faithful to that calling. To my great shame, I have not. But I am convinced that the really great issues before us will be settled on our knees. This does not mean (I repeat) that we should do nothing but pray; it does mean we should do nothing without praying. If it is true that God customarily uses means, it is no less true that we so often focus on the means that we forget that the really significant work must be God's, or the whole is to little avail. It may be that there are some Christians around who are so heavenly minded they are no earthly good; but I have met few of them. I know far more who are so earthly minded they are good for neither heaven nor earth.

Jesus' compassion issues in prayer, and in a call to pray. It may be that if we fail to pray, it is because our compassion is defective. Or it may be that our compassion is engaged, but our diagnosis of the problems and their remedies is faulty, prompting us to devote all our energies to what are at best secondary solutions. But if we align ourselves with the compassion of the Lord Jesus, and his analysis of the most urgent needs and their solution, we shall learn to pray to the Lord of the harvest that he will send forth laborers into his harvest field.

3. The compassion of Jesus issues in mission carried out by his disciples (10:1ff.). The call to prayer is central, but it is not everything. As faith without works is dead, so also is prayer without mission.

In some ways, of course, this mission was a training mission, and only in that sense was it a pattern for the continuing mission of the church. Luke reports a later mission that sent out seventy-two disciples (Luke 10:1–24) – apparently a growing group of trainees. The particular commission that Jesus delivers to the twelve apostles here in Matthew 10 preserves a number of features of relevance only during this pre-Passion, pre-Pentecost phase of outreach.[6] In particular, he tells them, 'Do not go among the Gentiles or enter any town of the Samaritans. Go rather to the lost sheep of Israel' (10:5–6). This restriction was probably advanced for several quite different reasons. Normally Jews and Samaritans did not get on very well; Jews and Gentiles could not be expected to get on any better. If (as I think likely) the foray Jesus makes into Samaritan territory, reported in John 4, had already taken place by this time, it may be that some of the disciples naively thought that everything would go swimmingly if they returned to Samaria. If so, they were unaware of the depth of their prejudices, or how difficult the task of proclaiming the kingdom could be; for a short while later, when some of the Samaritans reject Jesus and his followers, James and John at least are ready to call fire down from heaven on them (Luke 9:52–56), thereby demonstrating they are in no fit state to exercise a ministry in that region. Even after Pentecost, most of the believers, including the apostles, need some time before they are able to integrate a Gentile mission into their thinking.

Another reason for this temporary restriction may have been Jesus' understanding of his own place in redemptive history. He was sent as a Jew among Jews; he himself obeyed the law of Moses, and lived and died under it. When he ministered outside this framework, he himself seems to have seen it as something of an exception (e.g., see Matt. 15:21–28). This was a stage in the drama of redemption, a stage to be superseded in the great commission he himself would one day leave with his followers, commanding them to make disciples of all the nations (28:18–20).

Training mission or not, however, the first fifteen verses of this chapter nicely preserve a number of features endemic to all genuine Christian mission; and thus they contribute to our grasp of what Jesus' compassion really means. If Jesus' compassion issues in mission, we need to know something of the kind of mission we are talking about; and when we find that out, we shall learn something more about the nature of the compassion that prompted the mission.

(a) This mission is itself an extension of the saving reign of God. In the context of expressing his compassion, Jesus 'called his twelve disciples to him and gave them authority to drive out evil spirits and to heal every disease and sickness' (10:1). More explicitly, he told them, 'As you go, preach this message: "The kingdom of heaven is near." Heal the sick, raise the dead, cleanse those who have leprosy, drive out demons' (10:7–8*a*). Their *verbal* message was the proclamation of the nearness of the kingdom; their *deeds* were to display the power of that kingdom, delegated to them by Jesus, in powerful acts of healing, exorcism, and even raising some from the dead.

In short, then, their mission was to multiply the activity of their Master. The new age of his reign was being inaugurated. He himself was proclaiming the nearness of the kingdom (4:17); so would they. He himself was displaying the kingdom's power and anticipating what the consummated kingdom would be like (chaps. 8 – 9); so would they. He himself was rolling back the frontiers of suffering and making public connections between sin and sickness; so would they. He himself was confronting the powers of darkness and throwing evil spirits out of their human dwelling places; so would they. And they would do these things because he would delegate to them the authority they would need.

A few years ago that might have been all I would say on this passage, save that I would seek to apply it a little to the modern setting. As I prepare this today, however, the western church is feeling the impact of the so-called signs-and-wonders movement, usually identified with John Wimber and his associates in the various 'Vineyard' organizations. In brief, this movement holds that when the gospel is properly proclaimed, it should be accompanied by signs and wonders – that is, by an observable display of divine power in healing and other supernatural manifestations that attest and confirm the truth of the message that the kingdom is actually invading this world. This outbreak of power is often combined with 'words of authority' that seem to be a kind of subset of what older charismatics would have called the gift of prophecy.

It is not the place to assess so large and diverse a movement here, or to attempt an interpretation of the key passages on which the movement largely relies. In any case I have attempted something of the sort elsewhere. My purpose in raising the subject here is to acknowledge that the subject can scarcely be avoided in a context that plainly talks about Jesus' delegation of authority to his disciples, in the days of his flesh, in terms largely congruent with the categories used by the signs-and-wonders movement. At least some sort of brief reflection about the movement seems called for.

In fact, I find myself in large agreement with a lot of the statements that Wimber makes; and I have no desire to tear down another's work, especially where large parts of it seem wholesome, biblical, and on the whole helpful. If I must articulate a few cautions (which are better grounded in the book to which I have just referred), I would make the following four points.

First, although after Pentecost signs and wonders are performed by a wide variety of believers, they are rather frequently associated with the apostles (Acts 2:43; 4:30; 5:12,16; 8:18; 2 Cor. 12:12), sometimes as attesting acts. Of course, some today argue that the gift of apostleship has never been withdrawn; and so if apostles in the first century were in part attested by signs and wonders, their modern counterparts may be similarly endowed. This view does not adequately recognize the diversity of meanings that are subsumed under the word *apostle*. In one sense, Jesus alone is 'the apostle and high priest whom we confess' (Heb. 3:1): presumably no one claims to be an apostle in exactly the same way as Jesus is an apostle. Then there are the Twelve, who according to Acts 1 had to meet the condition of being with the other disciples of Jesus throughout his earthly ministry, and who were appointed to the task by Jesus himself (or in the case of the replacement of Judas Iscariot, by the church in solemn deduction from Scripture and drawing of lots). Again, there can be no modern counterparts to apostles in this sense, unless someone turns up who is at least a couple of thousand years old. Then there is Paul, who insists that among his qualifications is the fact that he saw the resurrected Jesus on the Damascus road and received his commission directly from him (especially 1 Cor. 9 and 15). Paul does not think of his experience on the Damascus road as one of many visions, but as qualitatively different: a special, final ('last of all,' he says, 1 Cor. 15:8) appearance of Jesus, in his resurrected form, an event not to recur until Jesus comes again at the end of the age. And further, there are apostles in a still broader sense: missionaries, envoys, messengers of the churches. In this broader sense, we may speak (as one book title does) of *Adoniram Judson*,

Apostle to Burma. But the frequent association of signs and wonders, I would argue, is with 'apostles' in the narrower senses. This does not mean that there is no valid display of signs and wonders today, nor that others than apostles (in this narrower sense) will inevitably find it impossible to display God's power. It does mean, however, that the frequent, biblical association of apostles with supernatural displays of kingdom power must not be denied, or cavalierly warped by identifying certain contemporaries as 'apostles' without carefully sorting out *in what sense* they are apostles.

Second, the emphasis on the inbreaking power of the kingdom of God must be balanced against other equally biblical emphases, including the prevalence of suffering in this fallen world. Not all deaths end in immediate resurrection: if the command to raise the dead (Matt. 10:8) were a universal mandate, it is rather surprising that none of the early Christians has survived to the present day. We have already noted that Paul first preached the gospel in Galatia because of an illness; he had to leave Trophimus behind in one mission, owing to a protracted illness; and Timothy had ongoing problems with his health. Even so-called natural disasters function, according to Jesus, as warnings to encourage people to repent (Luke 13:1–5). To this we must add the special emphasis in the New Testament on the inevitability of Christian suffering that stems from the world's opposition (about which I'll say more in the next chapter). To put the matter another way, to have no theology of the power of the gospel in our contemporary world is to relegate virtually all kingdom blessings to the return of Jesus – that is, it is to have an overemphasis on futurist eschatology. On the other hand, to place too much stress on the transforming power of the kingdom today, divorced from other competing and qualifying themes, is to depreciate what we are still waiting for, what the entire created order still groans for, the final redemption. It is to have an overemphasis on realized eschatology. After the cross and the resurrection, New Testament writers can say, in various words, that whoever calls on the name of the Lord will be saved; they do not say that everyone who calls on the name of the Lord will be healed from every physical illness. The church will remain in tension over how much power and how much weakness should characterize her until the consummation of all things.

Third, moreover, if this signs-and-wonders theology is treated as a kind of key to evangelism and mission, we are in for some weighty disappointments. With time, virtually all keys – whether the four spiritual laws, a certain style of evangelism (e.g., with altar calls), a particular theological emphasis – tend to become fetishes, the necessary means exploited by the faithful to produce inevitable results. Somehow God's work in regeneration becomes hostage to the particular key. Exercising the specified means becomes a test of orthodoxy. What begins as a salutary correction easily degenerates into a party position, with disproportionate energy devoted to the key and precious little to God or to people.

Fourth, perhaps most serious in this particular instance is the failure of the leadership to dissociate itself from some of the worst extremes of its followers. Obviously no leader can be permanently responsible for everything one of his students says or does; but in this instance there have been such remarkable excesses and abuses that some kind of clarification is urgently needed from the principal leadership. Historical examples flock to mind.

During the Evangelical Awakening, for instance, George Whitefield, the Wesleys, and other leaders were at first openly sympathetic to a group known to historians as the French Prophets. The French Prophets cherished supernatural phenomena, wild displays of emotional frenzy, utterances they claimed were from God, and so forth. The principal leaders of the Awakening wanted to be open to all that God might in fact be doing among them. But as the French Prophets became more and more extreme, cherishing their experiences and orientation more than the biblical framework and balance (even though they doubtless thought themselves to be biblical), Whitefield and the others eventually dissociated themselves increasingly from representatives of that movement, even on occasion administering public rebukes when the Prophets tried to take over the direction of a meeting. In short, there is ample evidence that the love of the spectacular can never be satisfied, and will issue in progressively serious distortions of biblical Christianity. When reports hit the media of Wimber protégés holding a gruesome vigil to bring back from the dead a believer who had been a cripple most of his life (Why wasn't he healed before he died?), it is time for some public dissociation.

Having said so many negative things, it is the more important for me to stress that not only this initial trainee mission of the Twelve, but also the entire mission of the church, is an expression of the compassion of Jesus Christ. The saving reign of God is being extended, sometimes in strange ways difficult to understand, sometimes in dramatic displays of life-transforming power, sometimes in the context of persecution and suffering, 'famine or nakedness or danger or sword' (Rom. 8:35). As Jesus' compassion moved him to incite his disciples to prayer, so his compassion moved him to train them for ministry, and to delegate some of his authority so that they too might preach the message of the nearness of the kingdom and display its power among the lost sheep of Israel.

(b) The discharge of this mission must never be for personal financial advantage. Jesus tells his followers, 'Freely you have received, freely give' (10:8*b*). The word *freely* does not here mean 'bountifully,' that is, 'You have received a bountiful supply, so give bountifully' or the like, even though that would have been true. Rather, it means gratis: that is, 'You have received without paying for anything, *freely*; therefore you must give *freely* as well, without charging for anything.'

Yet this does not mean Jesus' emissaries are not to be supported by those to whom they minister; for Jesus adds, 'Do not take along any gold or silver or copper in your belts; take no bag for the journey, or extra tunic, or sandals or a staff; for the worker is worth his keep' (10:9–10). Whatever the precise significance of this list, it is clear that the Twelve are to go stripped to essentials. The 'sandals,' for instance, may well be an extra pair that they are prohibited from carrying: such basic necessities they should expect to be provided for them along the way, along with the food and shelter that the gold and silver would otherwise purchase.

At first glance this might seem like a contradiction. On the one hand, the disciples are to give 'freely,' that is, without charging; on the other hand, they are to remember that 'the worker is worth his keep,' and travel lightly in the full expectation that their needs will be met by those to whom they minister. Why this tension between what appear to be competing or even mutually contradictory principles?

This strange arrangement makes good sense once it is clear what values are preserved by it. On both sides of the arrangement, we must consider the effect on those whom Jesus sends and those who receive them. That the disciples do not charge for their ministry forces them to remember that they, too, are the recipients of grace, and that spiritual treasures are not to be marketed in anticipation of the greed of Simon Magus (Acts 8). Those who charge for spiritual ministry are dabbling in simony. Meanwhile, those who receive the benefits from ministry freely bestowed are forced to consider that even by these strange means God makes it clear that his forgiveness and power cannot be earned, bought, or sold. The kingdom comes as he sees fit, when he sees fit; and when he displays his power in forgiveness, healing, and transformation, it is never because he has been coerced, bought, or domesticated.

Yet these people who receive the gospel of the kingdom want to respond in tangible ways; and so they provide food, shelter, and support for those who are primarily engaged in spreading the gospel. They recognize that considerable labor goes into the task the disciples have taken on. They reason that, although the gospel came to them freely, there is a profound sense in which they *ought* to pay for the work of those who brought them the good news of the kingdom. The worker is worth his keep. Meanwhile, those who are busy primarily in proclamation and ministry are reminded by the generosity of others that they do not stand alone, isolated heroes completely independent from the common herd. They may not be sure where their next meal or bed is coming from; they therefore trust God to provide what is needed, and learn that God in his mercy supplies their needs through other of his servants.

If we apply this to the modern setting, we would phrase it something like this. The church should not *pay* its clergy for services rendered, as if somehow ministers and others live by *earning* their keep. Pushed to the limit, this might almost suggest that a servant of the Lord is paid so much per prayer, so much per sermon, so much per hour of preparation, so much per counseling session with a distraught widow who has just lost her son, and so on. No, the church does not pay its ministers; rather, it provides them with resources so that they are able to serve freely. The church recognizes that those who serve in this way must be 'kept,' and are worthy of it. In practice, this means that the ideal situation occurs when the church is as generous as possible, the ministers do not concern themselves with material matters and are above selfish material interest. The worst situation occurs when the ministers are grasping and covetous, constantly comparing themselves with other 'professionals,' while the church adopts the attitude, 'You keep him humble, Lord, and we'll keep him poor.'

The particular side that needs special emphasis in any setting is the one the people of that setting are most trying to avoid. In general terms, the church needs to hear verse 10*b* ('for the worker is worth his keep') to be reminded of its responsibility, its debt; and the serving disciple needs to hear the same verse to be reminded of how the Lord will provide for him. The minister needs to reflect on verse 8*b* ('Freely you have received, freely give') to bear in mind that grace is always free, and that the service rendered must not be bought or sold, but distributed as freely and as widely as possible.

This particular arrangement continues, I would be prepared to argue, in the letters of Paul – although he adds some important wrinkles of his own that cannot be discussed here. The values embraced by this tension not only make the immediate mission possible, but also lay the groundwork for a view of Christian witness and an understanding of the nature of grace that belong to the very heart of the gospel. In the context of Matthew 10, they are an expression of the compassion of Jesus Christ, a reflection of what he understood the mission of the church should be.

But more, there is in these arrangements a wise reflection of the relationship between Jesus and his disciples. Jesus' attitude to his own disciples is full of grace, abundant in compassion. If they are peculiarly his, it is because, like Matthew, they have been called by him; if they are in some sense more whole than others, it is because Jesus has come to them in their sickness and transformed them. They did not earn his favor; they did not deserve his compassion. Can compassion ever be deserved? It may be desperately needed; but it cannot be deserved without destroying its essence. Yet at the same time Jesus makes *demands* on his disciples. That he is compassionate does not mean there are no demands on his followers; that he wins people by his grace does not mean they can simultaneously be his and unchanged. For although Jesus has not come to call the healthy, but the sick (9:12), it does not follow that he permits them to remain sick. What kind of compassion would it have been if, in the days of his flesh, Jesus had 'felt compassion' on the sick and then cured none of them? What kind of compassion would it have been if he came to call not the righteous but the sinners, and then left them to wallow in their sin? The truth is that the exercise of his compassion results in the *transformation* of individuals. If his compassion is not effective, it may be morally commendable sentiment; but it is totally useless, save as self-serving catharsis. Jesus' expenditure of compassion, of grace, issues in transformed people who *will* increasingly meet his demands and follow in steps of obedient discipleship. And if so-called disciples fail to change at least the *direction* of their lives, they are no disciples at all.

Thus, Jesus' insistence on a certain tension between the free dispensing of kingdom benefits and the obligation of the recipients of those benefits to provide for the

kingdom's messengers is far from being an arbitrary decision. It is a reflection of the deepest realities of the gospel.

(c) This mission results in a divided response (10:11–16).
Just because this mission is to be motivated by compassion does not mean everyone exposed to its message will
be won over. Far from it: it divides people.

The division, Jesus says, will begin when the disciples
arrive in any village and make arrangements to stay at
someone's home. 'Whatever town or village you enter,'
Jesus says, 'search for some worthy person there and
stay at his house until you leave' (10:11). The worthiness
of the person, in this context, is not measured by wealth,
personal charm, multiplied gifts, or moral superiority,
but by his or her reputation for being open to the ministry and emissaries of Jesus. The disciples are to find
out who is interested in supporting Jesus' outreach in
this way; such a person is worthy, and Jesus' followers
should go and stay there, without going from place to
place trying, perhaps, to secure 'superior' lodgings.
They are already superior if they are provided by someone who is worthy in this way.

And so the disciples arrive on this worthy's doorstep.
There they will find out if genuine worth abides here or
not. It may be, of course, that the disciples have been mis-
informed: perhaps no worthy person lives there. In his
instructions Jesus allows for both possibilities: 'As you
enter the home, give it your greeting. If the home is
deserving, let your peace rest on it; if it is not, let your
peace return to you' (10:12–13). The greeting *peace to this
house* (Luke 10:5) or the like was common in Jesus' day. In
itself it conveys nothing special in this context; but
because it is uttered by an emissary of Jesus to someone
who is allegedly interested in nurturing his cause, the
response to the greeting turns out to be critical. If the
householder turns out to be unworthy (i.e., not interested

in following Jesus or giving aid to his disciples), then the disciples should let their peace return to them – that is, they shouldn't stay. But the loss is not theirs. Those who receive Jesus' disciples receive him (10:40). The unworthy person is not simply rejecting a few disciples; he is rejecting the Jesus they represent. Their greeting of peace is of special value because of their relationship with him; and if they leave, taking their greeting with them, the home they thus abandon is impoverished incalculably.

Potiphar's home was blessed because of Joseph's presence (Gen. 39:3–5): how much more the home that harbors the apostles of Jesus the Messiah!

Rejection of the disciples of Jesus, *because they are his disciples*, therefore ultimately invites judgment, and that is true not only of the individual or home but even of entire towns: 'If anyone will not welcome you or listen to your words, shake the dust off your feet when you leave that home or town' (10:14). Pious Jews leaving Gentile territory and returning to the Promised Land might shake the dust of the pagan territory from their clothes and feet, a symbolic way not only of expressing thanks for a safe return home, but also of rejecting all that was seen to be pagan. For Jesus to apply this custom to Jews must have been deeply shocking. The emissaries of Jesus the Messiah are now treating certain Jewish homes and towns as essentially pagan, ignorant of God, threatened with judgment.

The judgment theme becomes explicit in the final verse of the section: 'I tell you the truth,' Jesus says, 'it will be more bearable for Sodom and Gomorrah on the day of judgment than for that town' (10:15). Sodom and Gomorrah, proverbial for wickedness (Gen. 19; Isa. 1:9; cf. Matt. 11:22–24; Rom. 9:29; Jude 7), suffered catastrophic judgment on account of their sin; but on the final day, Jesus insists, as much as they will be condemned, the homes and towns that rejected Jesus and his emissaries will face more fearsome judgment yet. The point is made in greater detail in the next chapter (11:20–24), and presupposes that our responsibility before God is related to the advantages and opportunities we have enjoyed. That is a perennially sobering perspective that stands over the western world, a threat that looms larger when self-interest and materialism squeeze out what we know to be a better way.

'But,' you say, 'I thought you were going to talk about the compassion of Jesus. Yet here you are threatening judgment and hell.'

The truth of the matter is that it is common in Scripture to find the love of God and the threat of judgment side by side. God so loves the world that he sends his unique Son, we are told (John 3:16); but a few verses on we are told that 'whoever rejects the Son will not see life, for God's wrath remains on him' (John 3:36).

'God demonstrates his own love for us in this: While we were still sinners, Christ died for us' (Rom. 5:8), Paul writes; but it is only this that guarantees we shall 'be saved from God's wrath through him' (Rom. 5:9). Elsewhere, John delights us with the words *God is love* (1 John 4:8,16); but he is quick to add, 'We love because he first loved us. If anyone says, "I love God," yet hates his brother, he is a liar . . . He who has the Son has life; he who does not have the Son of God does not have life' (1 John 4:19–20; 5:12).

It appears, then, that if we are to be faithful to Scripture, it is difficult to deal at length with the love of God without saying something about God's wrath. This is not because God's love and God's wrath are entirely symmetrical. Rather, it is because God's wrath, a function of his holiness when it confronts rebellion, is the environment in which we live and breathe: we are all by nature 'objects of wrath,' the apostle tells us (Eph. 2:3). What is marvelous is that this same God, who has every just cause to be angry, is nevertheless the God of love; and it is that love that sent his Son, that love that sent the disciples, that same love toward us today that 'compels us' (2 Cor. 5:14) to bear witness.

The exercise of Christian compassion in a lost, harassed, and rebellious world leaves behind a transformed people or an increasingly guilty people. Everyone who reads these lines will either be drawn more closely to Christ, or become increasingly guilty before him. There is no middle ground; for the mission of Jesus results in a divided response. But those who have tasted and seen that the Lord is good cannot but rise and sing:

> High beyond imagination
> Is the love of God to man;
> Far too deep for human reason;
> Fathom that it never can;
> Love eternal
> Richly dwells in Christ the Lamb.
>
> Love like Jesus' none can measure.
> Nor can its dimensions know;
> 'Tis a boundless, endless river,
> And its waters freely flow.
> O ye thirsty,
> Come and taste its streams below.
>
> Jesus loved, and loves for ever;
> Zion on his heart does dwell;
> He will never, never, never
> Leave his church a prey to hell.
> All is settled,
> And my soul approves it well.

William Gadsby (1773–1844)

6 (Matthew 10:16–42

The Divisiveness
of Jesus

'I am sending you out like sheep among wolves. Therefore be as shrewd as snakes and as innocent as doves.

'Be on your guard against men; they will hand you over to the local councils and flog you in their synagogues. On my account you will be brought before governors and kings as witnesses to them and to the Gentiles. But when they arrest you, do not worry about what to say or how to say it. At that time you will be given what to say, for it will not be you speaking, but the Spirit of your Father speaking through you.

'Brother will betray brother to death, and a father his child; children will rebel against their parents and have them put to death. All men will hate you because of me, but he who stands firm to the end will be saved. When you are persecuted in one place, flee to another. I tell you the truth, you will not finish going through the cities of Israel before the Son of Man comes.

'A student is not above his teacher, nor a servant above his master. It is enough for the student to be like his teacher, and the servant like his master. If the head of the house has been called Beelzebub, how much more the members of his household!

'So do not be afraid of them. There is nothing concealed that will not be disclosed, or hidden that will not be made known. What I tell you in the dark, speak in the daylight; what is whispered in your ear, proclaim from the roofs. Do not be afraid of those who kill the body but cannot kill the soul. Rather, be afraid of the One who can destroy both soul and body in hell. Are not two sparrows sold for a penny? Yet not one of them will fall to the ground apart from the will of your Father: Even the very hairs of your head are all numbered. So don't be afraid; you are worth more than many sparrows.

'Whoever acknowledges me before men, I will also acknowledge him before my Father in heaven. But whoever disowns me before men, I will disown him before my Father in heaven.

'Do not suppose that I have come to bring peace to the earth. I did not come to bring peace, but a sword. For I have come to turn

'"a man against his father,
a daughter against her mother,
a daughter-in-law against her mother-in-law –
a man's enemies will be the members of his own household."

'Anyone who loves his father or mother more than me is not worthy of me; anyone who loves his son or daughter more than me is not worthy of me; and anyone who does not take his cross and follow me is not worthy of me. Whoever finds his life will lose it, and whoever loses his life for my sake will find it.

'He who receives you receives me, and he who receives me receives the one who sent me. Anyone who receives a prophet because he is a prophet will receive a

prophet's reward, and anyone who receives a righteous
man because he is a righteous man will receive a righteous man's reward. And if anyone gives even a cup of
cold water to one of these little ones because he is my
disciple, I tell you the truth, he will certainly not lose his
reward.'

Introduction

In many societies, a polarized or sectarian stance is often
considered a sign of maturity, even of manhood. This is
true in large sectors of the population in Northern
Ireland, Iran, and Nicaragua. This is not to say that in
Northern Ireland everyone belongs either to the UDF or
the IRA, or that in Nicaragua everyone is profoundly
sympathetic to either the Sandanistas or the Contras.
Rather, it is to say that in these countries there are many
elements of society whose very raison d'être is bound up
with a polarized stance.

I am not of course referring to mere disagreement
over a policy or a political party. Every society knows its
disagreements. I refer rather to such polarized and
absolute disagreement that each side assumes an almost
revelatory stance, treating its own position as transcendental, absolute, and non-negotiable truth – with all
other views seen, correspondingly, as heresy, to be
damned or burned out.

It might even be argued that what is distinctive about
the 'civilized' western world is our degree of tolerance.
Nothing is so important it is worth fighting for, it seems.
Or is that really so? Is there *nothing* in our culture to
which we attach transcendental importance?

Some might nominate hedonism. Certainly millions of
men and women pursue hedonism with reckless energy.

In one sense, hedonism is their god. But no one ever dies in support of hedonism – in the practice of it, doubtless, but not in the support of it; that would be a contradiction in terms. Others might argue that materialism or the vague concept of 'progress' might be appropriate candidates. But although materialism has taken deep rootage in the soil of western culture, and sporadically surges forward with new momentum and power, most people treat it as a wonderful goddess worth pursuing but not worth dying for. After all, rising numbers of people are voicing their awareness of the finite resources on our planet. Perhaps 'small is beautiful' after all. And insofar as materialism is one form of hedonism, it is hard to imagine suffering for it.

If there is one underlying, deeply rooted position that is treated as of transcendental importance in western societies, I suspect it is the notion of pluralism. This does not simply adopt the stance that diversity is a good thing, but that in the religious and philosophical arenas no position has the right to declare another position wrong. That is pluralism's position: and that position is the only one exempt from criticism. The power of this stance came home to me a few years ago when I gave some lectures at an Ivy League divinity school. Not a few evangelicals had been attracted to this institution with its history of great learning, on the grounds that evangelicals were tolerated there. Every group represented in the student body, for instance, had its turn to organize and run a chapel service: liberals and conservatives, Roman Catholics (of various stripes) and Protestants (of various stripes), and even a representative from one of the tribes of Plains Indians with their essentially animistic faith. The student paper allowed all the voices to speak, so long as there was no criticism of another position. Only two beliefs, so far as I could see, were so sacrosanct throughout most of the student body that if anyone had the temerity to demur there was invariably a violent reaction. The first was the right of women to be ordained; the second was the moral acceptability of homosexuality. Those two points were not to be questioned; everything else was negotiable, and the diversity itself judged wholesome and enlightened. The great god Pluralism enjoyed praise without ceasing.

All this may seem not only more tolerant but far wiser, far more mature and civilized than, for example, the fanatical commitment found under the Ayatollah Khomeini's regime. But there is a high price to pay, too seldom recognized. First, pluralism, as I have already hinted, is surprisingly *in*tolerant. All positions *except its own* are negotiable. That is the great problem with most forms of liberalism: liberalism can afford to be liberal only to liberals. Others are dismissed as fanatics, bigots, narrow-minded hate-mongers, and so forth. Pluralism turns out to be as intolerant as the intolerant concoctions it condemns. Second, pluralism turns out to be the unwitting stooge of the contemporary social agenda. Because it is rootless in its values (except for the vague but powerful values of pluralism itself), it does not therefore abandon absolute values but tends instead to adopt as absolute those values at the top of the current cultural agenda. Hence my experience at the divinity school. That generation of students did not begin to suspect how much their values will appear to later historians to be the culture-bound hostages of the eighties. They thought they were on the leading edge of Christian truth; in fact they were on the trailing edge of a culture whose god is pluralism. And that brings up the third element in the high price paid by pluralism: it inevitably tends toward the depreciation of truth, even the possibility of knowing truth. The positions it then espouses are informed less by thoughtful criteria than by current fads. A position strongly held by those judged out of step with pluralism will be dismissed not on the basis of careful assessment but on the basis of the fact that it is out of step with pluralism. The truth-claims advanced by the position will never get a hearing.

Well, then, someone might ask, are we to return to the Crusades? Would we be better off with a world view that could renew the Spanish Inquisition? Should the church, claiming absolute truth, take the power of the sword and put matters to right?

God forbid! In the centuries that spawned the Crusades and the Inquisition, the church, true enough, had some genuine appreciation of the non-negotiability of truth; and that was commendable. But the church made other crucial errors. It aligned itself with the state – indeed, it declared itself so superior to the state that it utilized the sword of the state to enforce its wishes. It thereby failed to come to grips with the relationships between the old covenant people of God and the new. Under the old covenant the locus of the people was a nation, with a nation's laws; under the new, it is a transnational community, a minority, a frequently suffering fellowship, whose supreme sanction is excommunication. In the western world today, however, these costly errors are not so prevalent. The church is largely free from the state; and even where in the western democracies there is a state church, that church is largely free from the *power* of the state. Moreover, the force of circumstances is making it begin to understand, at least in some circles, its calling and role as a suffering community. But by and large the church has not yet grappled very hard with the non-negotiable character of truth, thoughtfully setting out the implications against the backdrop of the prevailing pluralism.

We may ask ourselves: What does the man on the street think of Jesus Christ? Probably rather little; but if pushed, our interviewee will either cite some credal formula learned in childhood ('Jesus is the Son of God,' or something similar), or else say something like, 'Well, I suppose he was a very good man who said and did a lot of good things. Wasn't he the one who taught the Sermon on the Mount – be kind and love your neighbor and the Golden Rule and that sort of thing?' Such a response betrays not only a rather reductionistic view of Jesus, but a sentimental approach to the Sermon on the Mount; for the latter contains not only the Golden Rule ('In everything, do to others what you would have them do to you, for this sums up the Law and the Prophets' [Matt. 7:12]), but also sweeping claims to authority on the day of judgment: 'Not everyone who says to me, "Lord, Lord," will enter the kingdom of heaven, but only he who does the will of my Father who is in heaven. Many will say to me on that day, "Lord, Lord, did we not prophesy in your name, and in your name drive out demons and perform many miracles?" Then I will tell them plainly, I never knew you. Away from me, you evildoers!' (Matt. 7:21–23).

In other words, even the Jesus of the Sermon on the Mount is a Jesus for whom the modern western world is woefully ill-prepared. How much less prepared is it for the verses before us – indeed, for the entire theme of the divisiveness of Jesus! How often are we likely to meet a man on the street who would define the mission of Jesus in terms of 10:34: 'Do not suppose that I have come to bring peace to the earth. I did not come to bring peace, but a sword'? The reason why our world is so unprepared for this theme is because of the pervasive influence of pluralism. So formidable is this influence on the popular mind that even Jesus has been recast as a prophet of this new god. The fact remains that the Jesus of Scripture bears little likeness to this new Jesus. The real Jesus, the authentic Jesus, the authoritative but compassionate Jesus, the Jesus who confronts the world, is quite frankly a divisive Jesus. This divisiveness is unavoidable, not only because of the unyielding truth-claims he makes for himself, but because at the heart of his message and purpose is his bold insistence that men and women can be rightly related to God only if they know him and come to him on his terms. This unabashed, exclusivistic, either/or mentality lies at the heart of the New Testament, and can be removed only by radical surgery on the documents. To resort to such devices because we are uncomfortable with the historical Jesus is merely another way of saying that we reject him in favor of a tame Jesus, a domesticated Jesus who will not challenge us or tell us we are wrong, force us to rethink our most fundamental assumptions, or question our most cherished priorities.

Four Features of the Divisiveness of Jesus

1. The divisiveness of Jesus leads to outright opposition from the world, and sometimes to persecution by it. When we remember what happened to Jesus, this first point should not be surprising. After all, as he reminds us, 'A student is not above his teacher, nor a servant above his master. It is enough for the student to be like his teacher, and the servant like his master. If the head of the house has been called Beelzebub, how much more the members of his household!' (Matt. 10:24–25). Beelzebub, or perhaps Beelzeboul, has an uncertain derivation. It may mean 'lord of flies,' a kind of god of filth, developed as a pun on 'Prince Baal.' Whatever the derivation, some pious Jews applied the word to the devil himself. Now the sobriquet is being applied to Jesus. If the matchless Son of God himself can be aligned in the minds of many with the devil himself, why should his followers think they will escape all opprobrium? Indeed, according to these verses the genuine disciples of Jesus will so attach themselves to the Master that they will be satisfied to be treated as he was. In that light it is not surprising that when the apostles first began to feel the heat of serious persecution, in the early years of the Christian church, they rejoiced 'because they had been counted worthy of suffering disgrace for the Name' (Acts 5:41).

This is of course nothing more than a reflection of the cosmic conflict between God and the order he has created but which now stands in rebellion against him. Sometimes those whose zeal for mission is informed less by knowledge than by enthusiasm tell us that there is a whole world out there waiting to hear the gospel. If by 'waiting to hear the gospel' they really mean 'needing to hear the gospel,' then of course they are right. But only rarely are people 'waiting to hear the gospel' in the sense that they are 'eager to hear the gospel.' When it happens there has invariably been some antecedent work of the Spirit of God, often through cultural and other pressures, that opens up a window of opportunity. Far more common is it to find genuine receptivity among a subset of the broader society, coupled with indifference or opposition from the masses.

In one sense, of course, Jesus was as concerned to prepare his disciples for ministry beyond the immediate mission as he was for this trainee mission itself. He was sending them out for this brief tour; but this mission was paradigmatic of their lifelong calling, and of the perpetual mission of the church. The opposition the apostles might face in the first instance was being shut out of someone's home, as we saw in the last chapter (on 10:11–15); but principally, Jesus was sending his followers out 'like sheep among wolves' (10:16). Down the road, they would face more vigorous attack; so Jesus warns them, 'But be on your guard against men; they will hand you over to the local councils and flog you in their synagogues' (10:17). What is in view is not the first mission – there is no evidence that the apostles faced flogging at this point – but the earliest years of the Christian church, before the irrevocable split with the synagogue had occurred. Synagogues often wielded discipline over their own members, and this included flogging with thirty-nine stripes. Once Christians had entirely withdrawn from the synagogue, of course, this punishment could no longer be meted out on them. But in many centers that breach was a long time coming. Paul himself suffered this flogging five times within the first two decades of his ministry (2 Cor. 11:24) – eloquent testimony to the persistence with which he himself practiced the principle that the gospel was 'first for the Jew, then for the Gentile' (Rom. 1:16).

But the Christian mission would not stop there. As Christian witness would one day extend beyond Judea and Galilee, and beyond the Jewish race, so too would the opposition: 'On my account you will be brought before governors and kings as witnesses to them and to the Gentiles' (Matt. 10:18). The words *governors* and *kings* indicate a non-Jewish environment; and the final phrase, 'and to the Gentiles,' makes this explicit. Over the centuries, these simple words have been fulfilled in vast arenas of persecution. Christians have been flogged, drowned, burned alive, racked, as well as suffering more esoteric punishments like having boiling oil poured down their throats, or being covered with pitch and set alight as human candles. Like the heroes of the faith listed at the end of Hebrews 11, 'the world was not worthy of them' (Heb. 11:38).

More commonly, Christians have not faced the ultimate trial, but have faced considerable harassment. When I was growing up in Quebec, it was not uncommon for a new believer to lose his clients once word of his conversion spilled out. In totalitarian regimes of the left or the right, Christians are often kept out of the best schools, restricted to certain menial types of employment, physically attacked, or simply shipped off to the local version of the Gulag Archipelago.

But this is part of the Christian's calling. The Master himself has said, 'I am sending you out like sheep among wolves' (10:16a). What a metaphor! The shepherd sends his sheep among the wolves! We are often treated to some artist's conception of Jesus the good shepherd rescuing his lost sheep – another use of the sheep/shepherd metaphor that obviously has many resonances for Christians. But I cannot recall having seen any representation of the strange imagery in this verse, even though it is clearly designed to help Jesus' followers get a handle on the nature of the mission to which they have been called. This is part and parcel of what Christian experience normally entails, and the point is repeatedly stressed in the New Testament (e.g., John 15:18 – 16:4).

How then should Jesus' disciples act? The metaphorical language turns to pick up two other creatures. We are to be 'as shrewd as snakes and as innocent as doves' (10:16b). In several ancient Near Eastern cultures, snakes were proverbial for prudence, shrewdness. But this virtue easily degenerates into cheap cunning unless it is married to simplicity, innocence. Doves are retiring but not astute: they can easily be snared by the fowler. Such innocence quickly degenerates into ignorance, even naiveté, unless married to prudence. Jesus' disciples must therefore be shrewd, prudent, avoiding attacks where possible, behaving wisely and with far-sighted realism; but they must also be innocent, open – not so cautious, suspicious, and cunning that they become paranoid, elusive, fearful. Doubtless the balance is difficult; but if we find it hard to articulate in the western world, it is because we have experienced relatively little opposition.

Clearly, then, the fact that the divisiveness of Jesus leads to opposition by the world, and sometimes to outright persecution, is no cause for either paranoid glee or rough belligerence among the people of God. Instead, it is cause for sober reflection, careful counting of the cost, wise assessment that fully expects trouble and is grateful when it passes us by. We are no better than fellow Christians in parts of the world where being a Christian can exact a high toll. Often we are less mature, because less tested. The *principle* laid down in this passage, however, is that we as disciples of Jesus should *expect* opposition, sometimes of the crudest kind, and view it as part of our calling. That is the way the Master went.

2. The divisiveness of Jesus extends to the disruption of families (10:21,34–39). In the first century, the words found in verse 21 would have been more shocking than they are to us – and they are shocking enough to us: 'Brother will betray brother to death, and a father his child; children will rebel against their parents and have them put to death' (10:21). Where the family unit is stronger than it is in most western democracies, there is corresponding horror at the thought of disruption. Ironically, it is often that very cohesiveness that can generate the betrayal of which Jesus speaks. In cultures with tight social units – Japan, or some Muslim countries – it is considered an extraordinary offense to do something that brings *shame* on the family. In such 'shame' cultures (as the cultural anthropologists refer to them), it can actually become a point of honor to take drastic action to remove the shame. Thus in some tightly controlled countries where Islam reigns uncontested, a family member who becomes a Christian brings shame on the entire family, and is therefore in serious jeopardy of being killed *by his own family*. It does not take much knowledge of Christianity in many non-North Atlantic countries to know how often conversion generates, as a by-product, the horrible betrayals and brutal violence of which Jesus warns us.

But let us not deceive ourselves. Although in the west we may not condone that degree of violence, we do not have to witness many conversions within our own culture before we discover painful examples of the family breaches that may ensue. Among personal acquaintances during the last few years who became Christians, three or four stand out for the price they paid in family relationships. A young Irishwoman placed her faith in Christ, and generated consternation among the members of her family when she shifted allegiance from the church of her birth. A Canadian university student, a Jew, became a Christian; his parents not only disinherited him, but held a funeral for him to symbolize how radically they were disowning him. An Englishwoman chose Christ at a British university, and her middle-class family felt deeply wounded – as if she were telling them that they were not good enough, or that they had not reared her properly. Several years elapsed before the breaches were healed. An American high-school student became a Christian, and went on to become a well-trained psychiatrist. When he decided to devote his life to training Christian ministers and missionaries, instead of pursuing one of the lucrative and prestigious practices or research posts he was offered, his wealthy father completely disinherited him.

Of course, these are more extreme cases; but few people who have become Christians as adults, and who come from homes with little sympathy for the gospel, have not faced some sense of serious dislocation. The truth is that we should not be surprised by this outcome. Jesus himself could define his mission in terms of such family disruption: 'Do not suppose that I have come to bring peace to the earth. I did not come to bring peace, but a sword' (10:34). Of course, he does not mean that his *primary* objective was division within families and larger units in society. He means, rather, that his firm commitment to his *primary* purpose, calling sinners to repentance (1:21; 9:13), inevitably results in lives so transformed in their direction and values that they will clash with the society from which they have emerged. Nor does Jesus mean that the consummation of the kingdom will bring perpetual strife and no tranquility. Rather, against many Jewish expectations that the kingdom would come in one climactic burst, Jesus insists that the kingdom comes in stages. The final climactic burst, the consummation, lies ahead; meanwhile, the inauguration of the kingdom brings stresses and division to a sinful world that cherishes its own self-centeredness. Such a world may pride itself on its high-sounding religious and ethical formulations; but in practice it is little prepared for the righteousness, forgiveness, and transformation of character the kingdom introduces.

The Old Testament analogy to which Jesus likens this situation is drawn from Micah 7:6: Jesus has come to turn ' "a man against his father, a daughter against her mother, a daughter-in-law against her mother-in-law – a

man's enemies will be the members of his own household"' (Matt. 10:34–35). In using words like these, Micah
the prophet was describing the gross sinfulness and
rebellion in the days of King Ahaz. As Jesus cites the
words, however, he claims he will actually *bring about*
these conditions: he has come *to turn* a man against his
father, a daughter against her mother. He does not mean
that those he wins as his disciples will turn against their
family members, but that by winning men and women
to himself their family members will turn against *them*.
Since that is the inevitable effect of his mission, and he
knows it, then in a sense he can say he has come to bring
it about. Moreover, since the disciples by following Jesus
and thereby attracting opposition actually align themselves with the prophets who were persecuted before
them (5:10–12), the disruptive wickedness in the time of
Micah the prophet points to the wickedness that erupts
with similar malice against Jesus' disciples.

But why must the gospel have such negative effects?
The reason is spelled out for us in the next verse:
'Anyone who loves his father or mother more than me is
not worthy of me; anyone who loves his son or daughter more than me is not worthy of me' (10:37). Of course,
anyone who dares say such a thing is either a maniac or
the Messiah. But even if we grant that Jesus really is the
unique Savior, Emmanuel ('God with us'), the virgin-
born Son of God Matthew presents to us, at first sight it
is still hard to make sense of this text. Why should Jesus
do something that is likely to weaken family ties? Isn't
he the one who elsewhere excoriates opponents for *not*
honoring their parents as they ought?

In fact, the text makes sense only if we have already
grasped two perspectives frequently found in the
Scripture. The first is that the entire world order is given
over to rebellion against God. Even the best of our social

institutions – our families, the best of our governments – are weighed down with self-interest that leaves no time for God, or only for a domesticated God. God's grace restrains such institutions and enables them to produce many wonderful things, to serve in many good ways; but so far as their orientation is concerned, they are not principally pledged to serve God our Maker, to please him in heart and in deed. Even when fairly high motives operate in these institutions, the *reason* for the motive is frequently not much more than mere utilitarianism. The second perspective is that the only way out of this dilemma, the only solution to our deeply ingrained self-interest, is conversion to Jesus Christ.

Within this context, the text makes sense; and indeed it can be applied beyond the family. Even when Caesar represents fairly good government, the new Christian finds his or her goals, priorities, and allegiances different from those of Caesar. If Caesar demands ultimate loyalty, the Christian must demur: he or she is sworn to another. Ideally, the Christian will still be, in many ways, an ideal citizen: honest, industrious, generous, law-abiding. But the Christian cannot focus all hope and expectation on the state, or a ruler, or a political party; and even if the Christian shares some of the hopes and aspirations of that party, final allegiance, ultimate confidence, and heart loyalty are devoted only to Jesus and his gospel. Exactly the same priorities are applied to family relationships. As warm, noble, and endearing a family as we may have enjoyed, unless it is profoundly *Christian* in its values it will primarily cherish things which, in their own way, are marks of rebellion against God: material prosperity, self-interested pursuit of status or reputation, dignity, cohesiveness. Some of these values are good, *provided* they do not become absolute, the organizing point around which life revolves. At that point, the family member who becomes a Christian must demur. Ideally, a Christian will do all that is possible to strengthen family ties and nurture this God-given institution; but a Christian will not yield top devotion, principal service, to the family or its values. Non-Christian members of the family sense this, and resent the conversion of the new Christian. The pressure is turned on; fundamental choices are demanded.

Sadly, it must be frankly acknowledged that some family problems experienced by new Christians owe a great deal to the spiritual immaturity of the convert. This Christian can cause needless offense. Even zeal for the conversion of family members can become a dreadfully insensitive triumphalism that breeds hurt feelings and deep resentments. But the naive zeal of a new convert is one thing; the sustained malice, suspicion, and even hatred of the rest of the family quite another thing.

Indeed, Christian conversion brings the new convert into conflict not only with the institutions of which he is a part, but with himself. For Jesus goes on to say, '... and anyone who does not take his cross and follow me is not worthy of me. Whoever finds his life will lose it, and whoever loses his life for my sake will find it' (10:38–39). The cross we are called to bear is not an individual affliction: migraine headaches, a bad marriage, difficult financial circumstances, a wayward child – all of them criticized under the frequently heard lament, 'We all have our crosses to bear.' We may all have individual burdens and difficulties to undergo; but that is not Jesus' point. Christians all have the *same* cross to bear: death to self-interest. In the Roman world, the person who picked up the cross-member and lugged it out to the place of execution had come to the end of hope. Only death was left. It was futile to plot new schemes larded with self-interest. And that is what Jesus means: he is talking about principal death to self-interest, and a new and principal commitment to himself.

The church needs to hear and proclaim this message afresh. Today we are bombarded with endless pseudo-Christian books to help us to become happy, content, resourceful, spiritual, successful, effective, creative. Even when these works convey considerable insight, the basic appeal is far too often, and far too deeply, to self-interest, covered over with the garnish of 'spiritual' language. The core truth is far simpler: 'Whoever finds his life will lose it, and whoever loses his life for my sake will find it' (10:39).

That is why this message is not full of gloom. The point is that, precisely because we were made *for* God, pursuit of *self*-interest is ultimately death-dealing; and for the same reason, when self-interest dies for Jesus' sake and is replaced by enthusiastic loyalty to him, the greatest spiritual irony occurs and we 'find' ourselves again.

That is why the happiest, most 'fulfilled' Christians are not those who know the most, or who criticize the most, or who analyze the most, but those who with right motives serve the most. If you seek fulfilment, you will not find it; if you seek to serve Christ, often in the countless loving deeds to others that are universally unacknowledged except in the ledgers of heaven, you will find yourself.

But all this goes against the grain of what Paul calls the 'natural man,' human nature devoid of transforming grace. We live in a world full of self-interest, some of it crude (rape, robbery, embezzlement, gossip, alcoholism), some of it sophisticated (climbing various social ladders, profound commitment to comfort, self-identification with parties and philosophies [whether good or evil] such that our identity is bound up with the party's progress). But Jesus Christ insists our only hope of escaping this morass, for now and for eternity, is to become his disciple, with supreme allegiance only to him. When that sort of conversion takes place, we are on a path quite at odds with our past, and even with our families. That is why the divisiveness of Jesus is inevitable where genuine conversions take place; that is why the divisiveness of Jesus extends even to the disruption of families.

3. The divisiveness of Jesus, and all the malice released because of it, are not to be feared. The passage before us offers five reasons to encourage us to overcome our fears.

First, persecution is not unexpected. All that I have said so far contributes to this point. Indeed, it becomes explicit in verse 26*a*. After telling us that the servant is not above his master, nor the student above his teacher, and therefore we ought to *expect* opposition from those who oppose our Teacher and Master (10:24–25), Jesus concludes, 'So do not be afraid of them' (10:26*a*). Fear is often stimulated by the unknown. But his followers, Jesus says, should *expect* opposition and persecution. Therefore if it breaks out, we should never be surprised; and by the same token we shall not live in dread of the possibility. If by God's grace we are spared serious difficulty, then we shall have all the more incentive to lift our voices to God in gratitude and praise.

This presupposes, of course, that part of the process of becoming a follower of Jesus has been the careful counting of the cost. If someone professes faith in Jesus, anticipating a life of uninterrupted bliss, spiritual victory, and considerable popularity, that person may become like the rocky ground in the parable of the sower (Matt. 13): 'But since he has no root, he lasts only a short time. When trouble or persecution comes because of the word, he quickly falls away' (13:21). But where there has been a careful evaluation of the cost, there can be little surprise 'when trouble or persecution comes because of the word.' Knowledge of this possibility largely reduces the fear.

Second, at crucial points we shall be granted special help. This is particularly true when the opposition takes on the cruder forms of persecution. 'But when they arrest you,' Jesus says, 'do not worry about what to say or how to say it. At that time you will be given what to say, for it will not be you speaking, but the Spirit of your Father speaking through you' (10:19–20). Gnawing fear can be more destructive than persecution itself; and in a totalitarian regime, high officials are likely to evoke far more terror than a corresponding official in a democracy where there is at least some possibility of redress. But Christians are not without unseen resources. Although Matthew does not major on the Spirit (unlike Luke), he elsewhere associates the Spirit with the kingdom's dawning (3:11; 12:28,31) and witness (28:18–20). The assumption here is that Christians, by virtue of the fact that they are Christians, will have been baptized in the Holy Spirit (3:11); and therefore if they face persecution they are to trust the gracious providence of a heavenly Father to provide through that indwelling Spirit just what needs to be said at that time.

This is not a text on which lazy preachers should rely, in the hope that inspiration will come as they enter the pulpit. They are not standing before persecuting tribunals (although they deserve to be!). Rather, this is the promise of direct help in the specific context of overt persecution; and because of this assurance, at least one of the fears associated with persecution may be laid to rest.

Moreover, the text does not absolve us from the obligation always to 'be prepared to give an answer to everyone who asks you to give the reason for the hope that you have' (1 Pet. 3:15). That should be part of the sustained commitment of every thoughtful Christian witness; and the older we get, the more we learn. Yet there is considerable comfort in knowing that the Spirit of God is with us even in our witness (cf. John 15:26–27) – the same Spirit of God who provides special assistance when our witness places us in serious jeopardy with the authorities.

Third, although opposition and persecution often occur in hidden ways not open to public scrutiny – not only the secrets of the torture chamber, but the candidate passed over, the quiet snubs, the backroom decisions – nevertheless all this takes place under the eyes of a God of whom it is said, 'Nothing in all creation is hidden from God's sight. Everything is uncovered and laid bare before the eyes of him to whom we must give account' (Heb. 4:13). That is why Jesus here says, 'So do not be afraid of them. There is nothing concealed that will not be disclosed, or hidden that will not be made known' (Matt. 10:26). Christians will be more willing to be despised for a time, if they consciously live in the light of eternity and what the judgment will reveal. The truth will not be concealed; all will come out.

In the same way, because this gospel we enjoy is destined to be known, we are bound to proclaim it: 'What I tell you in the dark, speak in the daylight; what is whispered in your ear, proclaim from the roofs' (10:27). The flat roofs of first-century Judea and Galilee made excellent platforms for orators. Jesus' point is that in certain ways his followers would have a more public ministry than he. There were certain things that he told only to them; in due course they would become responsible for making his teaching known as widely as possible. That obligation continues (28:18–20).

The truth must emerge; it will emerge. That includes both the hard realities of secret opposition and animus, and the glories of the gospel message: the truth will be made known. Living in the light of the end simultaneously encourages bold witness (because the truth of the gospel will prevail and will be recognized as God's truth), and quiet confidence in the face of opposition (because every facet of opposition to the gospel will one day be exposed).

Fourth, the wrath of God is more to be feared than the wrath of men. 'Do not be afraid of those who kill the body but cannot kill the soul,' Jesus says. 'Rather, be afraid of the One who can destroy both soul and body in hell' (10:28). The opposition's worst cannot be compared to God's worst. This is not so much an incentive to avoid all fear, as to ensure that fear is of the right kind, rightly directed. Doubtless Satan and his minions have great power (6:13; 24:22); but only God can destroy soul and body in hell. Small wonder, then, that 'the fear of the LORD is the beginning of wisdom' (Prov. 9:10), whereas the fear of men so often proves to be a snare (Prov. 29:25). If you fear God, you need fear no one else.

This is especially true because of the fifth reason put forward to calm our fears: God carefully watches over every detail of our life, not least when we are being vilely persecuted. God is not just to be feared; he is to be trusted. 'Are not two sparrows sold for a penny? Yet not one of them will fall to the ground apart from the will of your Father. And even the very hairs of your head are all numbered. So don't be afraid; you are worth more than many sparrows' (Matt. 10:29–31).

Jesus' argument is rather different from that put forward by many people today. They think that perhaps God is interested in the big issues, but find it difficult to believe that his sovereignty can extend to the tiny details of our lives. Jesus approaches the question of God's sovereignty by assuming that God's control over even the tiniest detail of the universe is absolute, and then draws comfort from the deduction that his care for larger matters must be correspondingly greater. If not a sparrow falls to the ground without his consent, should we suppose that his elect, redeemed at the cost of his Son's life, shall be of little concern to him?

This does not mean that we can rely on God's sovereignty to keep us out of persecution and difficulty. After all, Jesus has just told us that we should expect to face some opposition. The appeal to God's sovereignty is not to foster hope that we will be spared all difficulty, but to foster confidence that when those difficulties come we are not abandoned. Things have not fallen out of hand. We can still rely on the God who has permitted us to face these things to supply us with the grace and help we need to be faithful under such circumstances. Indeed, even beyond the question of persecution, it is the sovereignty of God, and the reliability of his covenanted love toward his own people, that enable Paul to assure the Corinthians: 'No temptation has seized you except what is common to man. And God is faithful; he will not let you be tempted beyond what you can bear. But when you are tempted, he will also provide a way out so that you can stand up under it' (1 Cor. 10:13).

These five reasons provide powerful incentive for allaying our fears when we contemplate the divisiveness of Jesus. Together they point to two further lessons that must not be missed.

First, our willingness to face opposition, and the cogency of the reasons advanced for not fearing it, depend utterly on a biblical Christianity that weighs everything from the perspective of eternity. If there is no heaven to be gained or hell to be shunned, if the forgiveness of our sins and reconciliation to God are not the most important things both for this world and for the world to come, then none of the arguments makes sense. Conversely, if these biblical perspectives constitute the fundamental realities of our existence, whether they are widely recognized in fallen human society or not, then it is folly to ignore them. What is sad to find is that form of belief that nominally assents to the existence of eternal realities, but does not act on that voiced assent. Such a tragedy is not merely inconsistent; it is dangerous. To put the matter another way: we cannot really see what biblical Christianity is all about until we live in the light of eternity. Only then do our responsibilities in *this* world come into sharp focus.

Second, in the light of these verses it is important to count the cost *both* ways. The expression *to count the cost* is regularly applied to the obligation would-be disciples have to weigh the nature of the potential opposition before forming a commitment. That is wise and right. But in the light of the blessings promised, and in the light of him who can destroy both soul and body in hell, would-be disciples are equally obligated to weigh the cost *if they ignore* so great a salvation. The calculation cannot be rightly made without considering eternity; it cannot be wrongly made if we are concerned to please him to whom we must still give an account fifty billion years from now.

4. *The divisiveness of Jesus characterizes Christian mission; but certain elementary truths soften the prospect and keep that divisiveness in perspective.* It is not just while becoming a Christian that painful opposition is sometimes experienced; it is also when *witnessing as a Christian* – that is, when engaged in Christian mission. In one sense, this is obvious; and it has already been made clear by a Lord

who tells his followers quite frankly that he is sending them out like sheep among wolves (Matt. 10:16). But if we focus on this point without keeping several elementary truths in mind, we are likely to become paranoid, gloomy, pessimistic, even (God help us!) masochistic – like certain cult missionaries who seem to extract a gloomy glee out of being told that they are not invited into our home.

What, then, are those elementary truths?

First, the need will always exceed the persecution. On the one hand, Jesus can say, 'All men will hate you because of me, but he who stands firm to the end will be saved' (10:22). 'All men,' of course, does not mean 'all men without exception,' or there would be no converts; rather, it means something like 'all men without distinction,' 'all men commonly' or the like. Even so, the prospect is daunting. But on the other hand, Jesus then hastens to add, 'When you are persecuted in one place, flee to another. I tell you the truth, you will not finish going through the cities of Israel before the Son of Man comes' (10:23).

Some of the details in this verse make it extremely difficult to comprehend. For reasons I have discussed at length elsewhere,[8] I think it is likely that the coming of the Son of man here refers to the destruction of Israel in AD 70. 'The coming of the Son of Man' and 'the coming of the kingdom' refer to the same event, though of course the first expression puts more emphasis on Jesus himself. But both expressions are ambiguous precisely because the kingdom comes in stages and the Son of man comes repeatedly. In one sense, Jesus is born a king (2:2); in another, the kingdom draws near when Jesus begins to preach (4:17). It has dawned when he casts out demons by the power of the Spirit (12:28); yet Jesus gains its full authority only after the resurrection – and even then, his reign is contested until he comes at the end and the kingdom is consummated (24:30–31). Even during the course of Jesus' ministry, the kingdom was dawning in both blessing and wrath (8:11–12; 21:31–32). Here in 10:23, the coming of the Son of man is that coming which makes it no longer possible to preach through the cities of Israel. It is that coming in which the judgment on Israel repeatedly foretold finally falls; and with it the temple cultus disappears, and the new wine necessarily takes to new wineskins (9:16–17). The new age comes into its own; the structured institutions that foreshadowed it are forced into oblivion.

In the immediate context of the disciples, that meant that as long as the nation existed they were not to permit persecution to engender defeatism or despair. If things became too explosive in one town – well, there were plenty of others that needed the gospel. The need would always be greater than the persecution.

The same principle has been invoked in various ways throughout the history of the church. Persecution may shut down one avenue of witness, but there are always others. Missionaries may be expelled from a country, many of the local leaders imprisoned or killed. But that does not necessarily spell defeat. The church may go underground, prosper, and multiply (as did the church in Ethiopia during World War II, or as has the church in China since the Revolution). Missionaries to China were reassigned all over the world, sometimes among large segments of the Chinese diaspora, carrying on fruitful work. The need will always exceed the persecution.

Second, our faithfulness in this mission is bound up with heaven and hell. Jesus insists, 'Whoever acknowledges me before men, I will also acknowledge him before my Father in heaven. But whoever disowns me before men, I will disown him before my Father in heaven'

(10:32–33). Paul similarly insists that a necessary criterion for being a disciple of Jesus is to acknowledge him publicly (Rom. 1:16; 10:9).

Of course, such acknowledgment will vary enormously from person to person. More may be demanded from a teacher or evangelist than from some others. Not all Christians are endowed with the same depth and maturity of faith. But after all the caveats have been entered, there is no Christian whom Jesus does not require to be a witness. In other words, it is impossible to forge an absolute disjunction between being a Christian and Christian witness. One cannot be the former without engaging in the latter.

Third, Christian truth is so crucial to the well-being of men and women that even how people receive Christian witnesses assumes a transcendental importance. That is the point of 10:40–42: 'He who receives you receives me, and he who receives me receives the one who sent me. Anyone who receives a prophet because he is a prophet will receive a prophet's reward, and anyone who receives a righteous man because he is a righteous man will receive a righteous man's reward. And if anyone gives even a cup of cold water to one of these little ones because he is my disciple, I tell you the truth, he will certainly not lose his reward.'

The same point is repeated several times in these verses to make it very clear. In verse 40, the apostles are in view: to receive them is to receive Jesus, and to receive Jesus is to receive God. In verse 41, the prophet and the righteous man are in view: the combination of the two terms elsewhere in Matthew (13:17; 23:29) points to Old Testament prophets, and the principle is again spelled out. If hospitality and help and general receptivity are extended to prophets and righteous men, not merely out of common courtesy but because of who these people are, there is a profound self-identity with what they stand for, a sharing in their commitments *and rewards*. John lays out the same principle, both negatively ('Anyone who welcomes him [the false teacher] *shares in his wicked work*' [2 John 11; emphasis added]) and positively ('Dear friend, you are faithful in what you are doing for the brothers, even though they are strangers to you. They have told the church about your love . . . We ought therefore to show hospitality to such men *so that we may work together for the truth*' [3 John 5–6,8; emphasis added]). We may not all be missionaries or pastors; however, if we receive such people, support them, identify with them, not because of ecclesiastical obligation, social pressure, or courtesy but because we are deeply identifying ourselves with what they are and do, we are sharing in their labors – and we will share in their rewards. The principle is so fundamental that it is extended to the ordinary Christian, 'one of these little ones' (to use the language of verse 42). If the courtesy of providing a drink is shown toward a Christian *just because he or she is a Christian, because he or she is a disciple of Jesus Christ*, the one who extends the courtesy is making an identification that will not lose its reward.

This, then, is the complementary truth to 10:11–15, which we examined at the end of the last chapter. If people receive us because we are Christ's, they are blessed; if they reject us because we are Christ's, they are in terrible jeopardy. That, too, is part of the divisiveness of Christ. But while we have been thinking all along of the difficulties aroused by Christian witness, of the opposition and even the persecution that may dog Christians' heels, it now transpires that those who oppose us are in far more danger than we. Just when some of us might have been feeling sorry for ourselves because of what might happen to us, we are now called upon to feel sorry for others precisely *because of* what they might do to us. That is the attitude that Jesus reflects when he cries from the cross, 'Father, forgive them, for they do not know what they are doing' (Luke 23:34) – an attitude Stephen, the first Christian martyr, adopted as well (Acts 7:60). Christian truth is so crucial that how others accept Christian witness assumes a fundamental importance. If this is borne in mind, our witness will be both bold and compassionate, and far less interested in our own welfare than in the welfare of those to whom we bear witness.

Conclusion

When Jesus confronts the world, division takes place. That is inevitable.

And when we think of the divisiveness of Jesus in the broader context of the nature of the world and the power of the gospel, we shall not be surprised – except perhaps by how little our faith has cost most of us. When we contemplate how much it cost Jesus, what eternal issues hang on the gospel, and how good and sovereign is the God who watches over our steps, we shall be the more willing to insist on the power and truthfulness of the gospel over against the prevalent pluralism. This insistence will not be sparked by spiritual pride, but by our knowledge of the Father through the Son. Because of him, we have found our sins forgiven and have learned to rest in the wisdom, grace, and power of God, both for our salvation and for protection and strength in the context of our growing discipleship and witness.

> We rest on Thee our Shield and our Defender!
> We go not forth alone against the foe;

Strong in Thy strength, safe in Thy keeping tender,
We rest on Thee, and in Thy Name we go.

Yes, in Thy name, O Captain of salvation!
In Thy dear name, all other names above:
Jesus our Righteousness, our sure Foundation,
Our Prince of glory and our King of love.

We go in faith, our own great weakness feeling,
And needing more each day Thy grace to know:
Yet from our hearts a song of triumph pealing;
We rest on Thee, and in Thy name we go.

We rest on Thee our Shield and our Defender!
Thine is the battle, Thine shall be the praise;
When passing through the gates of pearly splendour,
Victors we rest with Thee, through endless days.

Edith G. Cherry (d. 1897)

Endnotes

[1] The expression εις μαρτυριον αυτοις occurs in the Synoptics only here and at 10:18; 24:14; Mark 1:44; 6:11; 13:9; Luke 4:14; 9:5; 21:13.

[2] I discussed this, at least in an elementary way, in *How Long, O Lord?* (Grand Rapids, Baker Academic, 1991). The immediate context of the destruction of the swine provides at least a little perspective. He who is Lord of nature (Matt. 8:23–27) is also its ultimate owner, to dispose of it as he wishes (8:28–34). Apparently to banish the demons entirely would be to breach the 'appointed time' (8:29). Moreover the stampede of swine, whatever else it achieved, dramatically demonstrated that the demoniacs had been released (and what they had been released from!), and exposed the highest values of the surrounding people.

[3] The sequence of events in Matthew 9 is rather different from that in the parallels. I have discussed these relations at some length in my commentary on Matthew (in *The Expositor's Bible Commentary*, edited by Frank E. Gaebelein, vol. 8 [Grand Rapids: Zondervan, 1984]), pp. 220ff., and will not raise such matters here.

[4] I shall not here discuss the view, common in some quarters, that it is possible to know Christ's pardon without

displaying any evidence of its effect in one's life. This contemporary return to pagan perspectives, adopted in the name of defending grace and Christian assurance, understands neither grace nor assurance.

5 Judith Viorst, *Alexander and the Terrible, Horrible. No Good, Very Bad Day*, illustrated by Ray Cruz (New York: Atheneum, 1972).

6 Matthew 10 is a hotly disputed passage in New Testament research. In my larger commentary on Matthew (in *The Expositor's Bible Commentary*, edited by Frank E. Gaebelein, vol. 8 [Grand Rapids: Zondervan, 1984]), I have discussed at some length the literary, source, and theological questions surrounding this chapter, and I shall not repeat myself here. I shall also omit all mention of the individual apostles named in verses 2–4: these too are discussed in the commentary.

7 D.A. Carson, *Showing the Spirit: A Theological Exposition of 1 Corinthians 12–14* (Sydney: Anzea; Grand Rapids: Baker; Exeter: Paternoster, 1987).

8 D.A. Carson, *Matthew*, in *The Expositor's Bible Commentary*, ed. Frank E. Gaebelein, 12 vols. (Grand Rapids: Zondervan, 1984), 8:250ff.

New Carson Series from Authentic

Released Summer 2010, individually or as a boxed set

978-1-85078-892-8

978-1-85078-890-4

978-1-85078-889-8

978-1-85078-891-1

978-1-85078-890-4